Best of Breed

THE CAVALIER KING CHARLES SPANIEL

Your Essential Guide
From Puppy To
Senior Dog

Edited By **Maryann Hogan**

ACKNOWLEDGEMENTS

The publishers would like to acknowledge the following for help with photography: Pets As Therapy, Hearing Dogs for Deaf People, Maryann Hogan (Stavonga), Lucy Koster (Harana), Mark Sedgewick (Pacavale), Brian Rix (Ricksbury), Linda Flynn (Linjato), Alex Bubb (Wandris), and Jane Bowdler for outstanding archive material.

Cover photo: © Tracy Morgan Animal Photography (www.animalphotographer.co.uk)
pages 41, 46, 82 © Tracy Morgan Animal Photography; page 6 and 12 © istockphoto.com/Emmanuelle Bonzami
page 14 © istockphoto.com/Tomas Marek; page 38 © istockphoto.com/Nancy Dessel
page 51 © istockphoto.com/Chris Kridler; page 57 © istockphoto.com/Cameron Whitman
page 63 © istockphoto.com/dmorrisii; page 80 © istockphoto.com/Geoff Hardy;
page 81 © istockphoto.com/dmorrisii; page 98 © istockphoto.com/Eric Isselée;
page 97 © istockphoto.com/Emmanuelle Bonzami

The British Breed Standard reproduced in Chapter 7 is the copyright of the Kennel Club and published with the club's kind permission. Extracts from the American Breed Standard are reproduced by kind permission of the American Kennel Club.

THE QUESTION OF GENDER
The 'he' pronoun is used throughout this book instead of the rather impersonal 'it', but no gender bias is intended.

First published in 2008 by The Pet Book Publishing Company Limited
St Martin's Farm, Chapel Lane, Zeals, BA12 6NZ, UK
Reprinted 2010.
This edition published in 2014

ISBN
978-1-910488-04-1
1-910488-04-6

Printed and bound in China through Printworks International Ltd

CONTENTS

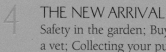

GETTING TO KNOW THE CAVALIER KING CHARLES SPANIEL

Chapter 1

The Cavalier King Charles Spaniel is the largest of the toy breeds. This charming little spaniel is a most striking dog to look at and commands attention wherever he goes. Invariably, when you walk out with a Cavalier at the end of the lead, people will stop you or smile as they pass by, and you will find that your Cavalier is always willing to greet people with a wagging tail. The Cavalier is an active, sporting breed and has a completely fearless attitude to life. He is friendly and outgoing, without a hint of nervousness or aggression.

The Cavalier was bred specifically to be a companion dog, and he does this job to perfection. He is loving and affectionate with his family and has a ready welcome for friends and visitors.

PHYSICAL CHARACTERISTICS

The Breed Standard, which is the written blueprint describing the 'perfect' Cavalier King Charles Spaniel, states that dogs should ideally weigh between 12 lbs and 18 lbs (5.4-8.2 kgs), but the Standard was written many years ago, and, in my opinion, Cavaliers are mainly at the top end of this scale now. Indeed, some of the top-winning show dogs are over 18 lbs (8.2 kgs). There is no height restriction given in the Breed Standard, but an ideal size is approximately 12-14 ins (31-36 cms).

As in any breed, there are, of course, dogs that will exceed the height and weight sizes, but the Cavalier should have the appearance of a small, compact dog. There is no way of knowing, when you buy a Cavalier puppy, how big he will be when he is fully grown, and there can be a wide variation. But when you go to buy your puppy, you should ask to see one or both of the parents, and from this you can usually get a good idea of what size the puppy will grow to.

This is one of the many reasons why it is so important to go to a reputable breeder to buy your puppy. A responsible, well-established breeder will be able to show you the mother of the puppies, and possibly the father as well. In many cases, you will be able to see other family members, and maybe even the grandparents and great-grandparents. In this way, you will see the type of Cavalier that is being produced, as well as getting an idea of size.

One of the main attractions of a Cavalier is his dark, melting eyes. The eyes should be round, large and very dark brown, spaced well apart, with a warm, soft expression. There should be

The Cavalier's heart-melting expression is a hallmark of the breed.

slight cushioning beneath the eyes, which helps contribute to the gentle facial expression. Once a Cavalier looks at you, you cannot resist him.

The face is framed by long ears, with plenty of feathering, which are set high on the head. The teeth should be strong, with a scissor bite, with the teeth on the upper jaw closely overlapping the teeth on the lower jaw. A young puppy may have an undershot mouth, which is when the bottom teeth are in front of the top teeth. This may come right as the dog matures. Cavaliers can also have an overshot mouth,

which is where the top teeth are a long way in front of the bottom teeth. This is often referred to as a parrot mouth, as it resembles a parrot's beak. Unfortunately, this will never come right. However, mouths are not a problem unless you intend to show your Cavalier.

A Cavalier's body should be short coupled, which means it is short between the last rib and the hindquarters. There should be a good spring of rib; this refers to the degree of curvature in the ribcage – in the Cavalier's case, it should be well sprung. The tail should be level with the back and be carried never much above the

level of the back when moving; it should be in balance with the body of the dog. The Cavalier should be free moving with plenty of drive from behind.

CAVALIER COLOURS
The Cavalier has a beautiful, long, silky coat, and there are four colours to choose from. These are divided into particolours and whole colours.

PARTICOLOURS
- **Blenheim:** A dog with Blenheim colouring has rich chestnut markings, well broken up, on a pearly white

PARTI COLOURS

Blenheim: Chestnut markings on a pearly white background.

Tricolour: Black and white with tan markings.

WHOLE COLOURS

Ruby: A rich red colour.

Black and tan: A raven black coat with tan markings.

Cavaliers are very sociable dogs and will live happily in a group.

background. Markings should be evenly divided on the head to leave room for the famous Blenheim spot. The Blenheim spot, referred to in the Breed Standard, is a lozenge-shaped mark on the top of the head, between the ears. This is unique to the Blenheim, and legend says that it is the mark of King Charles II's thumb print. Not all Blenheims have this mark; it is a bonus, but not essential.

- **Tricolour:** A tricoloured Cavalier has a well-spaced black and white coat, broken up with tan markings over the eyes, the cheeks, inside the ears, inside the legs, and on the underside of the tail.

WHOLE COLOURS

- **Ruby:** This is a rich red colour; white markings are undesirable.

- **Black and Tan:** A black and tan Cavalier has a raven black coat with tan markings above the eyes, on the cheeks, inside the ears, on the chest and legs, and on the underside of tail. Again, white markings are undesirable.

The colours are strikingly different, and people tend to have a preference for a particular colour. But it is important to remember that Cavaliers are the same shape and size, and have the same temperament, regardless of colour. You may not always get the precise colourings – for example, Blenheims and tricolours can be quite heavily marked, with less white – but this is just a cosmetic consideration. You may buy a whole-colour puppy with some white on his chest. This may disappear through time, and, unless you are

showing your Cavalier, it does not matter at all. Inheritance of colour is a complicated subject; suffice to say that two particolours cannot produce a whole colour, or visa versa.

TEMPERAMENT

The Cavalier temperament is second to none – once you have owned a Cavalier, no other breed will do. The hallmark is a complete soundness of temperament. This is a breed that is friendly with everyone, and has no tendency to nervousness or aggression. A Cavalier thrives on attention, and, before you know it, you've got a dog on your lap. A puppy may bite at your fingers, but this will be because he is teething, and, as with babies, he likes to chew. However, as soon as the second teeth have come through, the mouthing will stop.

The Cavalier will adapt to a home with children, or to living with older people.

Cavalier puppies love toys to play with, and this helps with teething and stops them chewing things they should not.

Cavaliers have a dislike of going out in the rain. My own Cavaliers do not want to go in the garden if it is wet outside. They stand at the door, look at the rain, and say, "No, thank you; we will wait a bit longer." Sometimes you have to literally push them out of the door to do their business – and they show such distaste for the wet, it is as though they are walking on hot coals. Funnily enough, when it is snowing, they love to go out and play in it; they run about, flicking the snow with their noses and trying to eat it.

Another trait in Cavaliers is their love of perching on cushions on the settee, behind your back, and draping themselves around you. One of my dogs used to stroke my hair with his paw. Some Cavaliers are born kissers, and, given the opportunity, will lick your hands, feet and face.

Cavaliers also love the company of other Cavaliers. The more the merrier is their philosophy, and they will play with each other all day. I often have people coming back for a second Cavalier; there is something in the breed that makes them addictive.

Generally, Cavaliers get on well with other breeds, but, like all dogs, they do need to be socialised. My Cavaliers live in the house, and consequently my puppies are used to the comings and goings of my family and grandchildren; before they leave me for their new home, they are usually well socialised. Puppies reared in kennels may not have the opportunity to see so many people, unless the breeder works hard at this aspect of rearing.

Most Cavaliers live quite happily with other pets. Several of my Cavaliers have gone into houses with cats – even some of the older Cavaliers I have rehomed – and they have settled down with their new feline friends almost straight away.

THE ADAPTABLE CAVALIER

In my experience, Cavaliers are happy in either town or country dwellings. The Cavalier is a family dog, and happy to live anywhere as long as he is with people who love him and feed him. Ideally, a dog should have a garden to run about in; otherwise, he will need extra walks. A Cavalier will also adapt to living in a flat, and, fortunately, he does not bark excessively.

If you have a large enough garden, it is a good idea to pave an area or put down a layer of pebbles in a separate plot. This means that when it is very wet, your Cavalier can go out without bringing lots of mud back into the house.

Cavaliers love children, and are usually very gentle with them. My dogs have been used to my three grandchildren since birth, and I have never had a moment's worry. My Cavaliers cannot wait for my grandchildren to visit, in the hope they will be taken for a walk or have their toys thrown for them. They fetch and carry extremely well, and are seemingly tireless.

Cavaliers make marvellous companions for older people. The Cavalier is very much a people dog and loves to sit on the settee, or preferably on your knee, and would stay all day if you let him. Cavaliers also love watching the television, and bark at any animal that appears on the screen. Although a Cavalier needs a certain amount of exercise, a run in the garden will suffice – Cavaliers are not mad keen to go out on a lead like larger breeds.

There is no better companion than a Cavalier: he is loving, but not too demanding, and fairly obedient in the home. Being a

Although the Cavalier is eager to please, he does have a mind of his own.

small breed, he is inexpensive to feed, as he does not need large meals. The Cavalier is not suited to long periods of time on his own, and so is an ideal constant companion for an older person.

Although Cavaliers are loving, they are very easy to rehome. A Cavalier will happily go off in a car, with a new owner, at any age, and settle down immediately. As long as he is loved and fed, he is happy. Many years ago, when we first moved to our current home, the front door blew open. I was upstairs and noticed my Cavaliers – I had eight of them at the time – wandering round several people's gardens. I quickly ran out and rounded up all but one. I put the rest away in the dog

room, grabbed a lead, and went looking for Glen, the one who was missing. As I rounded the corner, there was a lady with him on a lead. Apparently, she had been washing the car and had left the front door open. Glen had walked in the house, and she found him lying in front of her fire, with her Jack Russell. When she walked in the room, he just wagged his tail and continued to warm himself. I am sure that if she had not brought him back, he would have stayed there forever. A Cavalier is loyal to whoever is looking after him and feeding him at the time.

Cavaliers are extremely good travellers. Sometimes puppies can be car sick, but they usually get over it and your vet may be able to give you something to help. We have a caravan and travel many miles with our dogs. They love going away in the caravan, and get quite excited when they see us getting ready – they always seem to know when we are going away. The only downside is that they are great escape artists, and can get out of extremely small spaces, so we always take a large pen with us, which they go in if they are not with us in the caravan. A Cavalier on the run can be deaf to all calls.

A Cavalier will enjoy a long ramble, but is equally content with a play in the garden.

WORD OF WARNING

Cavaliers tend to put on weight quite easily. This is rarely a problem with puppies, but an adult can pile on the pounds unless food is carefully regulated. Do not allow your Cavalier to eat titbits between meals. If you are training your dog using treats, remember to deduct the food you use from his daily ration.

TRAINABILITY

Cavaliers are amenable and usually very biddable. They learn to be clean in the house quite quickly, as long as you remember to let them out after a meal and as soon as they wake up. They do need lead training, and I tell any buyer of puppies never to let small children take a Cavalier for a walk until he has been trained on a lead. Generally, small children run with a puppy on the end of the lead, and the puppy thinks this is the normal thing to do and starts running and pulling. This quickly becomes a habit that is hard to break.

The first time you put a lead on a puppy, he will probably sit down and refuse to move. It takes a lot of persuasion, and possibly some bribery. Walking in front with a treat in your hand sometimes helps. I usually take a puppy out with one of my adult Cavaliers, as the pup tends to follow the older dog. I have also found that puppies seem to walk better on grass to begin with. Once a puppy is fully trained on the lead, you can let older children take him out, providing they are taught how to walk the puppy correctly.

Every puppy needs to be taught good manners, such as how to greet and behave around people and other dogs. Most owners benefit from attending a good training class, where they can get used to working amid the distractions of other dogs. Your puppy will learn to focus on you, as well as having the opportunity to meet other dogs, people and children. With the correct training, your puppy will hopefully become a well-adjusted adult who is a pleasure to own. For more information, see Chapter Six: Training and Socialisation.

EXERCISE REQUIREMENTS

Fortunately, Cavaliers are very obliging when it comes to exercise. A Cavalier will gladly walk as far as you want him to go, or he will be quite happy just to run around the garden. I think that what a Cavalier likes best is to sit on the settee with his owners. However, you want your Cavalier to be fit and healthy, so regular exercise should not be neglected. I always tell prospective puppy buyers never to let a Cavalier off the lead unless they are in a safe environment.

Regardless of how well you have trained your dog, a Cavalier is easily distracted and has a tendency to run after the first thing he sees – and then becomes deaf to calls to bring him back.

Ideally, a Cavalier should have two walks a day to keep his muscles toned, but this little toy spaniel does not need the exercise that a larger dog would require. A puppy needs much less exercise than an adult dog. A good guide is to calculate approximately five minutes per month of age. By the time a puppy is four months old, he should be able to walk 20 minutes per day, which can be increased gradually. Remember to be a responsible dog owner, and take 'poo bags' with you. Some people give dogs a bad name because they do not pick up.

Exercise is a good way of keeping your Cavalier at the correct weight and making sure he is healthy. It has also been proved that dogs are very beneficial for your health, too. This is especially true for people with heart conditions and high blood pressure; the statistics state that patients are 50 per cent more likely to improve if they own a dog. Doctors will tell patients to exercise – and what better way to do this than by taking a dog out!

COAT CARE

A Cavalier puppy should be introduced to grooming at an early stage so that he gets used to the attention. The Cavalier has a long, silky coat, but it does not need extensive grooming. A couple of sessions every week should suffice. Do make sure that you check behind and under

Regular grooming will keep the Cavalier's coat in good condition.

A hearing dog forms a very close bond with his partner.

their ears, the top of the legs, and the feathering behind for knots, as they can appear from nowhere and be difficult to remove.

Cavaliers moult twice a year and it is essential that they are brushed more regularly at this time. Apart from preventing the coat matting, it does help to stop the spread of hair around the house. More brushing is required if you have your dog spayed or neutered, as they get a more woolly coat.

I find that regular bathing, using a dog shampoo and conditioner, followed by a thorough brushing, keeps the coat clean and healthy.

For more information, see Chapter Five: The Best of Care.

SPECIAL SKILLS

THERAPY DOGS

The loving, affectionate nature of a Cavalier Kings Charles Spaniel makes him well suited to working as a therapy dog. This is a scheme where volunteers visit hospitals, nursing and care homes, special schools, and a variety of other venues with their own pet dogs, who have been assessed as being calm and friendly.

These visits are of tremendous therapeutic value, bringing comfort and companionship to many residents of long-stay institutions who cannot keep a pet of their own. Children are sometimes referred to Pets as Therapy (PAT), which is the organising charity in the UK, when their fear of dogs prevents them from doing everyday things, like walking to school or playing in the park. The Phobic Children Project is a pilot scheme that helps children learn how to cope around dogs. By the end of the therapy, the children will be confident about coping with dogs, and be able to live a full life.

All PAT visitors and their dogs work on a voluntary basis. All new dogs must pass a temperament assessment and heath check. The dog must be fully vaccinated, wormed, and protected against fleas, and must have been in your ownership for at least nine months and living in your care. No special training is required, and you will be given helpful notes to assist you.

HEARING DOGS

Cavaliers can work as hearing dogs for deaf people and are trained for four to six months to alert people to sounds in the

The Cavalier's sweet and loving temperament makes him ideal for therapy work.

environment. They live in the homes of deaf people and are literally their ears. They learn to recognise seven sounds – smoke alarms, telephones, oven timers, alarm clocks, doorbells, door knocks, name calls – and alert their owner. They are also trained to help alert the deaf to sounds outside.

When a person who is hard of hearing or deaf takes his dog into public places, he or she will gain an awareness of the environment by paying attention to what the hearing dog is reacting to. When the dog turns to look at something he hears, the person will be able to see what is happening as well.

SEIZURE RESPONSE DOGS. These are dogs that are trained to help people suffering from epilepsy. Because of the differing needs of each other, every seizure dog receives specialised training. Tasks for seizure dogs may include, but are not limited, to:

- Summoning help, either by finding another person or by activating a medical alert/pre-programmed phone.
- Pulling potentially dangerous objects away from the person's body.
- 'Blocking' to keep individuals with absence seizures from walking into obstacles and other dangerous areas.
- Attempting to arouse the unconscious handler during or after a seizure.
- Providing emotional and physical support.
- Carrying information regarding the handler's medical condition.

Some dogs may develop the ability to sense an impending seizure. There have been some studies where dogs were trained to alert impending seizures by using a reward, but it is believed a dog either has this ability or lacks it completely. How dogs detect an oncoming seizure in a human is a mystery; they can warn people with epilepsy of an oncoming attack minutes, sometimes hours, before it occurs. This allows the person time to take medication, get to a safe place, or call for assistance. Potential seizure response dogs must be absolutely perfect for the job and must be capable of maintaining control in every situation. Because of the rarity of these traits, and the difficulty in training a seizure response dogs, only a few organisations provide them.

THE FIRST CAVALIERS

Chapter 2

There is no way of telling the origins of the Toy Spaniel, which has existed in different shapes and sizes for many hundreds of years. However, it is interesting to study paintings through the centuries. They feature in many pictures by the Old Masters as early as the 15th century. The Italian artist Titian (early 16th century) painted the *Venus of Urbino*, where there is a very small red and white spaniel curled up in a corner. This can be seen in the Uffizi Gallery in Florence. *The Medici Dogs in the Boboli Gardens* by Tiberio di Tito (right) shows spaniels wearing large earrings.

The story goes that most of the Kings of Navarre had pet dogs beside their hounds for hunting and coursing. Henry III of Navarre (1572) is reputed to have spent a small fortune on dogs each year. He had a number of these tiny dogs, which he carried in a basket round his neck with a wide blue ribbon. The dogs came from Smyrna, and were called Liline, Titi, and Miani. They mounted guard each night beside King Henry's bed. When a Jacobin monk came to St. Cloud to assassinate the king, the dogs had a premonition of evil. Liline, who

The Medici dogs in the Boboli Gardens.
Tiberio di Tito.

The children of Charles I and Queen Henrietta Maria. 1637,
Sir Anthony van Dyck.

Henrietta, Charles II's sister, with a
toy spaniel, c. 1665.

Charles II with his beloved spaniels.
Thomas Dankerts.

was usually peaceful and good-natured, leapt upon the monk, biting his ankles and tearing his cassock. In 1604 Henry had concluded a treaty with the Sultan of the Ottoman Empire, so perhaps the dogs were a gift from him.

In a tapestry to be found in *The Lady and the Unicorn Series* at the Musée National de Moyen-Age et des Thermes de Cluny in Paris, there is an instantly recognisable pale, slender spaniel with a very typical Cavalier head.

William Secord's *Dog Painting,* 1840-1940, is an excellent source of more recent paintings.

Charles I (reign 1625-1649) and his family had spaniels. *The Children of King Charles I of England and Queen Henrietta Maria*

1637 can be seen at Wilton House near Salisbury and shows the larger, snipier-nosed type. When King Charles II returned from exile on the Continent in 1660, he brought spaniels, and was remarkably attached to them. When the time came to name the modern breed, the choice of Cavalier was made in honour of him.

The diarist Samuel Pepys remarked that at a Privy Council meeting the King paid little attention to business but played with his little dogs. John Evelyn records: "The King took delight in having a number of little spaniels follow him and lie on his bed which rendered it offensive, and indeed the whole Court was nasty and stinking."

CHANGING TYPE

When William (1688-1702) and Mary came to the throne from Holland, they brought Pugs with them. The fashion for pet spaniels began to change, with shorter muzzles becoming more popular among the smaller dogs, but not the sporting Marlborough type. The Duke of Marlborough, hero of the Battle of Blenheim 1704, had a larger strain of red and white spaniels at home in Woodstock, near Oxford. They were very sporting after game and he said they should be able to keep up with a horse.

In *Diseases of Dogs*, 1832, author Blaine wrote: "Small yellow and white spaniels, which much resemble those known by the name of the Marlborough

THE BLENHEIM SPOT

The Duke of Marlborough's wife, Sarah, then Countess of Marlborough, was anxiously waiting for news of her husband away at the battle of Blenheim. She had an in-whelp pet spaniel on her lap and pressed her thumb constantly on the top of its head. When the puppies were born they all had spots on their head, now known as the Blenheim spot or lozenge, which has become a much-desired feature of the breed.

The Blenheims were well known for their gaiety and sporting instincts. *The Sportsman's Review* 1820, said: "The very small, or carpet spaniels, have exquisite noses and will hunt truly and pleasantly."

Charlie, a Blenheim Spaniel, showing the famous Blenheim spot.
Champion Dogs of England **by George Earl.**
Kind permission of the Kennel Club Library.

TOY SPANIELS

George Stubbs (1724-1806).

Gipsy and Fairy, the favourite spaniels of Paul, Lord Methuen. Exhibited at The Royal Academy, 1846. William Barraud (1810-1850).

breed, are very common amongst the Spitalfield weavers, who, coming from France, knew the correct type." Queen Victoria was devoted to her pet spaniel 'Dash', who was given to her when she was 13 in 1833. The most famous portrait of Dash was painted by Landseer and does not differ much from our present dogs.

In the catalogue of the National Exhibition on 1860, a Blenheim was shown by John Stretch of London. The dog had no name, but was by Mr Blaydon's Eclipse, dam Guppys Rose. Price £52. This was a lot of money for those days, particularly when, 85 years later, my mother, Amice Pitt, paid

15 guineas for Daywell Roger – and that was the going rate.

In 1885 The Toy Spaniel Club was formed, and four colours were recognised:

- King Charles: black and tan
- Prince Charles: tricolour
- Blenheim: rich chestnut or ruby red markings on a pearly white background
- Rubies: rich chestnut red.

There were shows and matches throughout the 19th century, but, by the 1920s, the longer-nosed Toy Spaniel had ceased to exist, apart from those kept at Blenheim Palace, near Oxford.

The short-faced King Charles

were officially named as a breed by the Kennel Club in 1903, and it was not until 1945 that Cavaliers were officially recognised and registered by the Kennel Club, but more of that later.

TOY SPANIEL REVIVAL

The catalyst for restoring the old type of Toy Spaniel was an American philanthropist called Roswell Eldridge from New York. He must have been a great anglophile, as he came over to England for the fox hunting. He was disappointed when he failed to find an English Toy Spaniel as seen in the historical paintings and was told they no longer existed. In 1926 he gave two

George Morland (1763-1804).

Lady Hamilton (1758-1805).

prizes at Crufts for £25 to be awarded to the Best Dog and Best Bitch of the variety described as "old fashioned Toy Spaniel with a long nose".

In 1924, a very clever (if experimental) dog breeder called Miss Mostyn Walker, living in Norfolk, had bred two puppies of extreme Cavalier type out of a noseless bitch called Ann, supposedly by the Blenheim stud dog Lord Pindi. There is some doubt about this and a possible Papillon sire was mentioned. She was not trying to breed the old-type spaniel but wanted to create Pocket Cockers. The two puppies went on to become the legendary Ann's Son and Whizbang

Timothy. Ann's Son stayed with Miss Mostyn Walker, and Timothy became the property of Mrs Fincham. Of the two, my mother, Amice Pitt, found Timothy to be the better foundation sire.

Miss Mostyn Walker was a genuine breeder with a very good knowledge of what she was trying to do. She mated Ann's Son to a short-faced bitch called Nightie Nightie. This resulted in a Blenheim bitch, called Nell, who became the property of Major and Mrs Brierley, and a dog called Duke's Son. Daywell Nell later became the mother of Ch. Daywell Roger.

In the same year, my mother

became involved with Toy Spaniels. She already had a large kennel of Chows and her kennel name was Ttiweh (my father's name, Hewitt, reversed). In 1924 she bought a small, noseless, ruby dog puppy from Mrs Higgs, a King Charles breeder, as a present for her mother. This puppy was Master Robert, a most charming and comical little dog. Unfortunately, he had fits due to a bad bout of distemper and was unsuitable as a present, so she kept him. Later, she went back to Mrs Higgs who, this time, sold her a Blenheim bitch called Waif Julia. Sadly, no photograph exists of this bitch. As my grandmother was not ready for a puppy then,

Dinah: A 'nosey' King Charles of the 1920s.

Amice Pitt's first toy spaniel from King Charles breeding.

my mother took Waif Julia down to Miss Brunne, a well-known breeder of short-faced dogs, to be mated. Miss Brunne immediately suggested that Waif Julia should go to Crufts, entered in the class for the old-fashioned type. My mother then recognised that Julia was the perfect example of the old Marlborough spaniel with its retrousse nose, beautiful even markings, and clear lozenge-shaped spot in the middle of the head between the ears. She took Julia to Crufts and, as Miss Brunne had prophesised, won the special prize in 1927. Imagine the indignation of the King Charles breeders when these exhibits, literally their chuck-outs, qualified for these large prizes.

Ann's Son won the prize every time he was shown in 1928, 1929, and 1930. At some stage

Miss Mostyn Walker sold him to an actress for £100. But she left him shut in her dressing room when she went on stage, and, when she returned, found he had torn the upholstery apart. Luckily, he was swiftly returned to Miss Mostyn Walker and lived happily ever after with her.

THE FIRST BREED CLUB

With this success at Crufts came the idea of forming a breed club. The first meeting was held on the second day of Crufts Dog Show in 1928. It was decided by the toss of a coin that Miss Mostyn Walker should be president and chairman, and Amice Pitt was to be secretary and treasurer. The vice presidents were appointed and, in all, eight members of the new club were present. The subscription was 5 shillings. The

name chosen was the Cavalier King Charles Spaniel Club.

Neither Miss Mostyn Walker nor Amice Pitt were amateur enthusiasts, as Miss Mostyn Walker had bred various toy breeds. My mother shared her father's interest in genetics, and she had successfully bred and exhibited Chows for some years. She devoted the rest of her life to improving and furthering the cause of the Cavalier.

Her father, Sir Everett Millais (eldest son of the Pre-Raphaelite artist Sir John Millais), studied at the Pasteur Institute in Paris, doing research into rabies. He was also interested in the breeding of livestock in general and wrote a book called *The Theory and Practice of Breeding to Type*, which was the standard work on the subject for many years. On the

BLUEPRINT FOR THE BREED

At the first meeting at Crufts, the Breed Standard was drawn up – it was practically the same as it is today. It was agreed that: "The dog should be guarded from fashion and there was to be no trimming. The perfectly natural dog was desired, and was not to be spoilt to suit individual tastes, or as the saying goes, 'carved into shape'. This gives an amateur with a good dog an equal chance when competing with professional handlers and trimmers."

Ann's Son was put on the table and chosen as the ideal type. Members brought reproductions of pictures from the 16th, 17th and 18th centuries, including several by Gabriel Metsu and other Dutch and Italian artists, showing an elegant, medium-sized dog with a shallow stop, well-placed ears and a flat top to the head (i.e. not apple-headed).

There was some misunderstanding over the type because the painting chosen to illustrate the Crufts catalogue over the breed entries was the well-known Landseer painting *Cavaliers Pets*, showing two spaniels lying down. This picture was not chosen to illustrate the desired type, as those dogs were considered to have too deep a stop and did not have the required flat skull.

AT STUD

FEE 3 gns. prepaid return carriage extra

"Ann's Son"

The Noted King Charles Spaniel.

NEVER BEATEN.

Winner of the £50 Trophy and £15 Special at Cruft's 1936, also winner of the £25 Special offered for Old Type King Charles Spaniels at Cruft's 1928, 1929, and 1930.

A very beautiful little dog.

Sires small stock of unmistakable type and quality

Miss Mostyn Walker,

Clova Kennels :: Costessey, Norwich.

TEL: COSTESSEY 76

A stud advertisment for Ann's Son, a winner at Crufts in three successive years.

Ann's Son: He was chosen as the 'ideal' when the first Breed Standard was drawn up.

EARLY CAVALIERS

Peter of Ttiweh 1928.

Bridget of Ttiweh.

Puppies of the early 1930s.

Rangers Bimbo, Bridget of Ttiweh, and Mary Ann of Ttiweh.

Jane Pitt pictured with Cavalier puppies in the 1930s.

practical side, one of his hobbies was dog breeding, and he was the first person to import Basset Hounds into England from France. My mother certainly inherited his interests and talents, although he died when she was an infant.

FIGHT FOR RECOGNITION

In the early days there was no support from the Kennel Club, apart from advising that owners should register as many puppies as possible in preparation for the time when they could apply for separate registration.

In Amice Pitts' words: "In the 1930s the Cavalier Club Committee invited two members of the Kennel Club to inspect their best specimens, placing them on the table next to a short faced Champion. To our horror, the Kennel Club said they could not see enough difference to warrant dividing the two types! This was a big disappointment to us, but having once determined to establish this breed we continued in our efforts."

Pioneers were often accused of using other breeds as outcrosses. In the 1940s one kennel produced a litter of very long-faced puppies, with liver-coloured noses and light eyes, and were strongly suspected of using a Dachshund. Many of the King Charles kennels produced a lot of dogs, with noses about one inch long, and the Cavalier owners used to buy these dogs and were delighted to get them. The breeders called them throw-outs and had no use for them. The one with the best head, owned by my mother in the 1920s, weighed 42 lbs, but was considered worth breeding from because of his head. When he was bred from, he produced the flattest-faced puppies ever seen, but as Amice said: "That is what breeding is all about – a lot of hit and miss; you have just got to go on trying."

In the paper *Dog World*, dated 18 January 1929, the King Charles correspondent wrote: "Everyone thought the movement to establish the Cavalier would fizzle out." They reckoned without my mother, who had taken up the matter with such vigour that there are now 10 Cavalier King Charles Spaniel Clubs throughout the UK, a separate Breed Standard recognised by the Kennel Club (1945), with 22 classes for the breed at Crufts (2007). Plus, the breed consistently has the highest number of toy dogs entered at Championship shows in the UK – and on occasion the highest number of dogs entered in the whole of the Championship Show!

INFLUENTIAL BREEDERS
In 1935 Daphne Murray (of the Crustadele prefix) came to help with the Ttiweh kennels, and so began a lifetime friendship. By that time Amice had about 60 Cavaliers, and still some Chows.

For the next few years, progress was slow and Kennel Club recognition was still withheld. As there were no Challenge Certificates, few people were sufficiently interested to try to raise a breed with no sales value. The original breeders persevered. Among them was Mrs Jennings, who started the Plantation kennels in 1926. Mrs Jennings was one of the main exhibitors during the 1930s, and in 1946 judged the first Club Championship Show.

Madame Harper Trois Fontaines originally bred Pyrenean Mountain Dogs, and came into Cavaliers in the 1930s. Her kennel name was de Fontenay, and she bred many winners. She bought her first bitch, Snow White, from Amice Pitt.

Other notable pre-war breeders were Mrs Speedwell Massingham of the Loyaltyway Cavaliers; Mr Vernon Green of the Astondowns; Mrs Maud Sawkins of the Greenwich kennels; Mrs Stoves, who owned the great foundation sire, Cannonhill Richey; Mrs Katy Eldred of the Turnworth prefix; her sister, Mrs Daphne Murray, of the Crustadele prefix; Mrs Joyce Green of Heatherside; her sister, Miss Phyllis Mayhew, of the Mingshang kennel of Cavaliers

Cannonhill Richey: A foundation sire for the breed.

27

Amice Pitt with Ch. Daywell Roger and Ch. Abelard of Ttiweh.

The Hillbarns clan of tricolour Cavaliers.

and Pekingese; and Mrs Vera Rennie with the Veren kennel.

In the early 1930s, it was difficult to get classes at shows, as the Kennel Club was not prepared to recognise the breed. The Cavalier breed club approached various canine societies (The Ladies Kennel Association, Richmond Dog Show and Metropolitan and Essex Dog Show) to put on classes for the breed, with the club or individual members acting as guarantors.

No shows had classes for Cavaliers, so these early breeders travelled miles, entering their dogs in Any Variety classes and slowly building up the registration numbers, and getting them recognised by all-rounders.

THE BREAKTHROUGH

In 1939, as the war loomed, there was the heartbreaking task for kennels of all breeds: having to put down perfectly healthy dogs, as feeding non-productive animals was forbidden. We found homes for as many as possible, and most breeders managed to keep a few dogs. We took two Chows and two Cavaliers to live in the New Forest. The Cavaliers were Tinkle and Angelina of Ttiweh, but my mother did not breed from them, and some generous people gave homes to breeders' dogs to try to keep the lines alive.

The Kennel Gazette, January 1945, reported: "On December 5th, the General Committee agreed to a recommendation to grant a separate register for

Cavalier Spaniels, and to make Regulation 2 of Regulations for Classification read: Toy Spaniels – King Charles and Cavalier Spaniels. It was also decided to add these breeds to Regulations for Preparation of Dogs for Exhibition."

In 1945 Amice Pitt wrote to the Kennel Club, asking if the committee would alter the name of the breed to Cavalier King Charles Spaniels. The committee agreed. The committee then decided that Mrs Amice Hewitt Pitt, Mrs Eldred (then secretary of the club), and Madame Harper Trois Fontaine should be asked to discuss which dogs could be taken from the King Charles registers and could be appropriately known as Cavaliers. As a result of this, these ladies all

CHAMPIONSHIP SHOW STATUS

The committee applied to the Kennel Club for Championship Show status, and it was granted in May 1946.

Our first Championship Show was held on 29 August 1946. A wonderfully exciting occasion, it was held at Avoncliffe, a large house near Stratford-on-Avon, owned by Mrs Louise Hitchings of the Avoncliffe prefix. The house was used as theatrical 'digs' for the Royal Shakespeare Company and the onlookers at the show included many breed fanciers as well as actors who were fascinated by the strange goings on.

Mrs B. Jennings (Plantation) was the judge. There was an entry of 121 made by 38 individual dogs and three litters in 16 classes.

The Best Dog was Daywell Roger. He only managed a third prize in the Puppy, Blenheim or Tricolour class, beaten by two bitches, but although only 10 months old, he won Open dog, beating Mrs Rennie's very good black and tan Royalist of Veren, and the well-known Plantation Banjo, owned by Madame Harper Trois Fontaines: both infinitely more mature than him.

The first Championship show 1946.
Katie Eldred with Belinda of Saxham (left) and Jane Pitt (Bowdler) with Daywell Roger (right), who went on to become the first Champion in the breed.

met at the Kennel Club and pored through several large books of King Charles Spaniel registrations. Their job was to pick out the names of all dogs that were Cavaliers or Cavalier type, and they also included the names of King Charles Spaniels of both sexes that were known to produce 'nosey' puppies. From that list they compiled a list from which every Cavalier in the world today is descended.

Because of the very small gene pool, in the early days it was permitted to breed a Cavalier to a short-faced King Charles and register the puppies as interbred. Then, after two generations of breeding back to a Cavalier, the progeny was once more eligible for the Cavalier register.

Cavaliers were not awarded Championship status until 1946, and until then were shown in mixed classes with King Charles Spaniels.

A NEW BEGINNING

As soon as the war ended, my mother started looking for a dog puppy to join the three bitches we already had. We found

Ch. Royalist of Veren: The second black and tan Champion in the breed.

Ch. Little Dorrit of Ttiweh with Jupiter Mars and Mercury, sired by Ch. Daywell Roger. Jupiter went on to become a Champion.

Daywell Roger born 7 October 1945. It was a great excitement to find a dog so closely related to Ann's Son. His sire was Cannonhill Richey, but over to my mother's words:

"He was bought unseen as the nearest dog to Ann's Son I could obtain, with no idea of him becoming a Champion and certainly no hint of his potential as a stud dog. He arrived and failed to impress – a rather stocky, stuffy puppy with a curly coat, but with the loveliest expression. Huge dark round eyes, with tremendous generosity and courage. He cost the very moderate sum of fifteen guineas. His character and temperament were perfect. Fearless, jolly, dominant but never quarrelsome. He had enormous influence on the kennel, keeping a fatherly eye on all the other inmates. Fights or possible fights between the stud dogs were immediately checked by Daywell Roger just walking over and intimating he would not allow such behaviour. As a stud dog he needs no boost from me. He seemed to be able to get the best from all the bitches sent to him. His record is all down on paper, as anyone who studies pedigrees can see. The first Champion in the breed, his line has continued right down the generations. His last litter, sired when he was 12 years old, produced Britannia of Ttiweh, the dam of Ch. Cerdric of Ttiweh who won the Stud Dog Cup in 1964 and 1965."

In 1936 Mrs Joyce (Bunty) Green and her sister, Miss Phyllis Mayhew, had admired the Cavaliers at Crufts, and they wasted no time finding some after the war. Mrs Green founded the Heatherside kennels, and Miss Mayhew added them to her already flourishing Mingshang kennel of Pekingese. Mrs Green owned Ch. Mingshang Sir Roger, Ch. Heatherside Andrew and Ch. Heatherside Anthea whose dam was Daywell Amber, sister of Daywell Roger. On two occasions Ch. Heatherside Andrew won the

Cup for the Best Head under Amice Pitt and myself.

Mrs Massingham, Madame Harper Trois-Fontaines, Mrs Jennings, Miss Grant Ives, Daphne Murray and Katie Eldred had all kept the breed going during the war, and were soon back where they had left off.

There is no record of any club business between 1935 and 1945, but Kennel Club records show that 60 Cavaliers were registered between 1940 and 1945.

THE BREED DEVELOPS

It was a normal sight at shows all over England to see Mrs Pilkington and Mrs Pitt arriving with at least six or more dogs each to boost the entries – certainly not all of show quality – which must have posed many problems for the judges. History was made in 1948 when Daywell Roger gained his third CC, becoming the first Champion of the breed. I well remember my pride that day. The judge was Tom Scott, a well-known all-rounder.

In 1947 the minutes show that Mrs Keswick had joined the club. She bred Cairn Terriers before the war and was to play a big part in the development of the breed. Mrs Joyce Green also joined the club that year. Mrs Keswick bought her foundation stock from the Avoncliffe and Ttiweh kennels, and it was not long before she produced her first Champion, Ch. Pargeter Jollyean

Ch. Crisdig Leading Seaman: A fine representative from the Crisdig kennel.

of Avoncliffe (born 21 May 1947), by Ch. Daywell Roger out of Avoncliffe Heatherbelle.

The first black and tan Champion was Ch. Amanda Loo of Ttiweh, born in 1946. She still holds the record for winning the most Challenge Certificates for a black and tan. The second black and tan Champion was Ch. Royalist of Veren, born in 1945, and owned by Mrs Rennie.

The second Championship Show was held in 1947 with Mrs Florence Mitchell judging. She was a well-known King Charles breeder. Madam Harper Trois-Fontaines won Best of Breed with Ena de Fontenay, and the dog CC

was won by Mrs Jennings with Plantation Smut. There were 150 dogs entered, which was a remarkable achievement.

The Kennel Club granted two shows in 1948. At the first show, Daywell Roger gained his title; the second show was at Hinchwick, a beautiful Cotswold house near Stow-on-the-Wold, which belonged to Mrs Pilkington. Mr Walter Worfolk, an all-rounder, was the judge. The Best in Show was Mrs Eldred's Belinda of Saxham, winning her second CC, and the dog CC was won by Robin of Veren owned by Mrs Vera Rennie.

In 1949, Miss Pamela Turle bought Lucasta of Sunninghill from Mrs Pitt. The sire was Daywell Nimrod of Ttiweh and the dam was my ruby Victoria of Ttiweh. Lucasta was the grandmother of tricolour Ch. Aloysius of Sunninghill, who went on to win 19 CCs, which was a record he kept for many years.

CAVALIER SPECIALISTS

The 50s was a notable decade, bringing in many members who were very keen and did a lot for the breed. Sir Dudley and Lady Forwood went to a show at Ascot and fell in love with Cavaliers. Their first was Lustre of Bletchington, a present from the Hon. Mrs Astor, and their second was a Ttiweh from Mrs Pitt. Lady Forwood went on to breed many Champions.

Ch. Dickon of Littlebreach: This Cavalier was thought by many specialists to be a near perfect example of the type required by the Breed Standard.

In the early 1950s, Colonel (later Brigadier) Jack Burgess and Mrs Susan Burgess started the Crisdig kennel, buying two half-sisters from Mrs Burroughes. A landmark for the breed came in 1951 when Mrs Pitt won Best in Show at the South Eastern Toy Dog Society. In 1952 a Cavalier won the Toy Group at the City of Birmingham Show.

The following year John Evans and Alan Hall answered an advertisement for a spaniel. They were then gundog people and were expecting to see a Cocker. It turned out to be a Cavalier of the Astondowns breeding, which was a lucky start. They then bought Crisdig Molly Malone, a daughter of Ch. Crisdig

Celebration, from Colonel and Mrs Burgess. They later made breed history in 1973 by winning Best in Show at Crufts with Ch. Alansmere Aquarius.

Also in the early 1950s, Mrs Pares-Wilson (later Lady Daniel) started her Cocklehill Kennel with two puppies from Mrs Keswick, Pargeter Gretel and Pargeter Rupert, becoming President of the Club from 1970-75.

At the Club AGM in 1955, it was announced that 380 Cavaliers had been registered the previous year. This was the highest to date and meant the Cavalier stood fourth in the Toy Group.

Mrs Pamela Estcourt started

her Alemap kennel in 1958, and the same year Mrs Diana Schilizzi started her Chacombe kennel with Bowstone Paul, bred by Mrs Irene Booth. Mrs Peggy Talbot (Maxholt) bought his litter brother. Later Mrs Percival gave Venetia of Little Breach to Mrs Schilizzi who went on to win 8 CCs in one year. She was the dam of Ch. Chacombe Alexis. Mr and Mrs Schilizzi are always very hospitable, allowing their lovely grounds to be used for various club events and parties.

Mrs Amy Nugent of the Tregun kennels in Ireland and her husband, Raymond, had a kennel of 50 racing Greyhounds, which they trained and raced. In 1960, Mrs Nugent bought her first Cavalier, a tricolour from Mrs Bartels. Also in 1960, Mrs Nesta Follows and her son, Paul, joined the club. Their first bitch was Pargeter Fuss, litter sister to the more successful Pargeter Flip.

The club continued to grow with notable names, such as Mr Rainy Brown in 1960. In 1961 Mrs Jane Booth and her husband Maurice (known to his friends as Bod) bought Millstone Jade of Ducks Cottage from Mrs K. White.

Miss Molly Marshall of the Kormar kennels specialised in whole colours. She bred Ch. Don Miguel of Kormar (1958), sired by Ramon of Kormar. Ruy Evanlyn of Kormar was the sire of Ch. Cordlelia of Chacombe and Ch. Ivan the Terrible of Chacombe.

Homerbrent and Homeranne Champions (left to right): Caption, Carson, Carnival and Festival.

John Evans pictured in 1973 with Crufts Best in Show winner Alansmere Aquarius.

Mr and Mrs Roger Stenning of the Cherrycroft kennel owned Ch. Dickon of Littlebreach, bred by Mrs Percival, and they also bred Ch. Cherrycourt Wake Robin. Roger was treasurer of the club for many years until he became chairman in 1975.

The mid-1960s saw new members who were to add to the strength of the club. Mr and Mrs David Williams, Mr Michael Harvey and Miss Harvey, and Mrs Jean Kent did a lot for Cavaliers in the south.

In 1964, Brigadier and Mrs Burgess produced the first club yearbook for Cavalier King Charles Spaniels – this annual publication continues today.

In 1966 Mrs Molly Coaker bought her first dog from Mrs Mary Kiser – Harrowbere Unity, a bitch by Croupier of Ottermouth. Her first Champion was Ch. Lindy Lou. Many Champions followed from the Homerbrents or Homeranne dogs, owned by Mrs Coaker's daughter, Anne Reddaway, including Ch. Homeranne Caption and Ch. Homerbrent Pentilly, both winning 13 Challenge Certificates.

In 1963, Mrs Mary Cryer won the Toy Group at Crufts, with Ch. Amelia of Laguna. She was bred by Miss Lila Mackay, who also bred Whippets. She was by Ch. Aloysius of Sunninghill out of Pargeter Paprika. In the same year, Miss Parker (now Mrs Lesley Jupp) joined the club. Her first dog came from Lady Forwood's Eyeworth kennel, then she bought Eyeza Crisdig Pip from Mrs Burgess and made him a Champion. Mrs Jupp then became club secretary; she ran the Championship Show for 11 years and in 2005 became chairperson.

In 1964, Mrs Diana Maclaine started the Lochbuie kennel with dogs from Miss Pamela Turle, Sunninghill and Mrs Daphne Murray Crustadele. She was on the club committee from 1971, then secretary for 14 years from 1976 before handing over to Mrs Jupp. She bred International and Scandinavian Champion Trademark of Lochbuie.

Mr and Mrs Tom Boardman started the Volney line with a Sunninghill dog, then a black and tan from Mrs Jane Booth

Ch. Ricksbury Royal Legend: Dog breed record holder up to December 2007.

rounder judge Mr Vivian Bennet. Best opposite sex was Mrs Susan Burgess's Ch. Crisdig Florida. Alansmere Aquarius went on to win the Toy Group, then Best in Show, under judge Mr Owen Grindey who had been at the original Championship show in 1946. This was a wonderful day and led to a greatly increased popularity for the breed. Ch. Alansmere Aquarius's sire was Ch. Vairire Osiris, and his dam was Ch. Alansmere McGoogans Maggie May. He already had one Challenge Certificate and between Richmond 1972 and Bath 1973 won seven consecutive CCs, thereby achieving his Championship.

The current breed record holder changed in 2008 with Ms Alex Bubb's homebred Ch. Wandris Entertainer winning 35 CCs. He is sired by Ch. Pascavale Enchanted out of Wandris Show Girl.

There are so many leading breeders from the past who deserve to be mentioned in this chapter but are not. It is more of a personal memoir and I hope it will encourage you to look back and find a lot more information on the people who did so much for the breed.

The interest in Cavaliers is still increasing. There is The Cavalier Club and 10 regional Clubs in the UK. In 2007 the registration with the Kennel Club was 11,422.

(Millstone). Their first Champion was Ch. Crisdig Peace of Volney.

Mrs Diana Fry started her Amanta kennel with a bitch, Huntsbank Cascade, from Mrs and Mr David Williams. Then came the Blenheim bitch, Helen of Aquasulis, who lived to 18, bought from the Aquasulis kennel. Sanubray Georgina, bought from Mrs Barbara Spencer, was next to join the kennel, later followed by Chandlers' Arabella from Mrs Vera Preece. In 1974 Mrs Fry won her first CC with Bohemian Rhapsody.

Brian Rix and Kevan Berry of the Ricksbury kennel began in

1970 and their foundation bitch was Crisdig Saucy Sue, by Ch. Crisdig Leading Seaman, out of Ch. Crisdig Cornish Caper (from which all their current Champions descend). This team went from strength to strength, winning BOB at Crufts four times – with Ch. Ricksbury Royal Legend winning BOB on three consecutive occasions. To date the Ricksbury kennel have held four breed records (one of which they still hold), and have made up 20 UK Champions, plus numerous Champions overseas.

In 1973 John Evans took his 17-month-old dog, Alansmere Aquarius, to Crufts. He won best of breed under the all-

EXPORTING TO THE USA

Mrs Vera Rennie exported the first Cavalier King Charles

Ch. Wandris Entertainer: Current breed record holder with 35 CCs.

Spaniel recorded in the United States in the late 1940s. This was a dog named Robrull of Veren, who went to Mrs Harold Whitman of Bedford, New York.

Toy Spaniels appeared in paintings in America as far back as 1696, in a remarkable picture entitled Captain Kidd in New York Harbour. In this picture, discovered by Mrs Garnett-Wilson of the Laughing Cavaliers in America, Captain Kidd – the famous privateer-turned-pirate – is welcoming ladies on board his ship with a medium-sized well-marked Blenheim in the foreground.

Mrs Barbara Keswick was another breeder to export to the US. She sent several good dogs to Miss Elizabeth Spalding of Maine, who won Best in Show at the Inaugural Show of the American Club with Pargeter Lotus of Kilspindie.

The US Cavalier King Charles Club was founded in 1956 with Mrs W.L. Lyons as its first president. The first show was held in 1952 at the home of Mrs Lyons Brown (her sister-in-law) in Kentucky.

In the USA, the show scene for Cavaliers is more complicated than in the UK. The

breed was not recognised by the AKC until 1996, becoming the 140th breed to gain official recognition. There is now the American Cavalier King Charles Spaniel Club Inc., and the 'old' club, the CKCS USA, which operates outside of the AKC jurisdiction with regard to approval of judges, registrations of progeny etc. Both clubs have a number of regional clubs that report to their main club for approval of issues. Exhibitors may exhibit in both clubs, but need to register their dogs with both in order to compete in each camp.

A CAVALIER FOR YOUR LIFESTYLE

Chapter 3

Think long and hard before taking on the commitment of owning a Cavalier.

You have now made the decision to have an addition to the family, and decided it is to be a Cavalier King Charles Spaniel. So what do you want from your Cavalier? Different breeds have different characteristics, and the Cavalier King Charles Spaniel is a dog that excels at being a companion and thrives on human companionship. A Cavalier enjoys being around other animals, but human contact and attention is essential. He is great in a family environment or as the sole companion to an elderly person. He will take as much exercise as he can get – but is not over demanding and will adapt to the limitations that today's environment imposes. A Cavalier is best in a home where he is not left for more than three to four hours a day maximum. He is

The Cavalier is a superb companion for young and old alike.

eager to please and is a great buddy for young and old alike.

It is not difficult to understand why the Cavalier is one of the most popular breeds in the UK. The handsome appearance, beautiful colours, adorable expressions, and endearing temperament have won the breed many admirers. The Cavalier is also a handy size for the house; he is generally sound and sturdy, without the fragility of some of the other toy breeds. The Cavalier is a sporting spaniel in miniature.

BEFORE YOU BUY

Make sure that you have chosen the right breed for your needs; a Cavalier will be no good if you want a guard dog. But most important of all, remember that any dog, no matter what breed, demands a huge degree of commitment. Hopefully, you are looking forward to many years of companionship, and that also means care and financial commitment in terms of feeding, vet bills, suitable accommodation, good fencing, boarding kennels during holidays, and personal one-on-one time.

You also need to bear in mind the fact that your Cavalier will not always be a puppy and will, one day, be old and need support. You therefore need to be aware of the possible ailments your Cavalier might succumb to.

The aim is to purchase a well-bred and healthy specimen that is typical of the breed, with all the breed characteristics you desire.

So are you up to the commitment? Is there room in your life for a Cavalier? Given that your answer is 'yes', the next step should be to contact your local breed club/society; details are available from the Kennel Club (see Appendices). The Kennel Club will put you in contact with the breed club secretary and/or the puppy register run by the society. Through this contact, you will be given details of members of the society who have puppies available in your area. These breeders have, hopefully, abided by the society's Code of Ethics; they should have carried out all the necessary health checks and reared the puppies using best practice and with all the love and care you would expect.

DOGS AND DOG CARERS

When you make contact with a breeder, you need to understand that he/she will want to find the best possible home they can get for their precious puppies. So do your homework and be prepared for lots of questions about why you want a Cavalier, what your needs are, and what pet experience you have.

A conscientious breeder would never sell a puppy to a household where there is nobody at home all day. This means a sad life for a dog, with no companionship; the dog gets bored, which leads to destructive behaviour in the house, and the owners wondering what has gone wrong. Sometimes it is possible that the dog will spend the day with the 'in laws' or parents, and be collected in the evening. This arrangement can work, but a breeder would want to ensure that this is a permanent arrangement, and that the daytime carers know what is involved, so the puppy has a secure and regular regime.

Older dogs might be content with a dog walker calling in once or twice a day, but for puppies needing socialisation and house training, and for energetic young dogs, this is not enough.

Where the prospective buyers are part-time workers or shift workers, then dog ownership is possible, but the work schedule of the buyers would be one of the breeder's first concerns.

LIVING WITH CHILDREN

If the prospective owners have children, or the puppy is being bought for a child (they cannot legally own a dog until they are 18 years of age), then there are further questions:

- How old are the children?
- Do they realise that puppies are not toys to be mauled and manhandled?
- Do they understand that a puppy cannot be abandoned when boredom sets in, or left at home when they go out to play with their pals?

Children and Cavaliers make a great mix as long as a sense of mutual respect is established.

Older children can appreciate the responsibility involved in having a puppy in the family, and, given the right environment, breeders will sell puppies to households with older children and teenagers. Often the child and dog become inseparable and form a very special relationship. However, there are too many instances where parents buy a dog for the children, who quickly become bored with the new addition and the dog is seen as a nuisance. The owners are not prepared to give the puppy the time they need, and the longed-for pup is, all too soon, looking for a new home.

DAILY ROUTINE

Whatever your daily routine was before acquiring a Cavalier, it will change once you have one. Do you have time in your daily schedule to care for your Cavalier's basic needs? That means at least two walks a day, time to feed the dog, train and play with him, plus time for socialisation.

Then there is the weekly routine. A Cavalier does not need a lot of grooming, but it must be done at least once or twice a week, with regular baths as an extra requirement. Remember that Cavaliers mean hair – and that means dog hairs in the house, which results in extra cleaning. A point to bear in mind when choosing the colour of your Cavalier is the impact this will have on your home and your clothes. Light hairs on dark suits are a menace, particularly if your Cavalier is to be allowed on the furniture.

SENIOR CITIZENS
At the other end of the spectrum, you may be a senior citizen looking for a companion. At the time of buying a puppy, you may be fairly independent but advanced in years, so you need to think what would happen to your beloved dog in the event that you are unable to care for him at some time in the future. Is there a close family member who would be prepared to take on the responsibility of your dog? Perhaps you could make an arrangement with family members that they contact the breeder and/or breed club to ask

for help and support in finding an alternative home if required.

You will probably find that most reputable breeders will be keen to ensure that they fully understand your situation, and proper provision is made for the future of your pet. The last thing the breeder wants is for the dog they placed in a permanent loving home to be passed from one person to another – who may not be interested, or indeed capable, of the commitment needed for your pet.

THE COLOURS
The Cavalier comes in four

colours (see Chapter One).

Ruby and Black and tan are not as readily available as Tricolour and Blenheim puppies, so you may have to look a little harder and book your puppy a good time ahead. Reputable breeders often have a waiting list for their stock.

You need to understand that when you see a puppy in the nest, he will not be the colour of an adult dog. Look at the mother and father for an indication of the final density/richness of colour. You will find that some of the markings on the particolours (Blenheim and tricolour) will change over time, with the colour taking over more of the white. In whole colours (ruby, and black and tan) a puppy may sometimes have a few white hairs on the chin, toes or chest. Depending on the extent, these few white hairs will often disappear by the time the puppy is an adult.

DOG OR BITCH?
An important question for some people is the sex of their puppy. Sometimes it boils down to a personal whim, or the buyers may say 'we have always had a dog' or 'we prefer the temperament of bitches'. This is

The four colours (left to right): Tricolour, Black and tan, Blenheim and Ruby.

very much a personal choice, but there are some factors to consider:

BITCHES

They come into season every six months or so, and this means there are extra considerations. An in-season bitch will need to be confined for perhaps three or four weeks. She cannot be allowed her usual freedom on walks in case she attracts the unwanted attention of the neighbourhood dogs.

The first 10 days of a season are sometimes a little messy, with the bitches losing colour (bloody discharge), so she will require a little extra sponging down, or grooming. There are many products on the market to minimise odours and inconvenience, so it need not be a big barrier.

You might be tempted to breed a litter for yourself (a decision to be taken very seriously), and no, bitches do not need a litter just for the sake of experiencing motherhood. You need to do extensive homework and understand bloodlines and a whole host of

other health and hereditary issues before going down that avenue.

Spaying a bitch is not necessarily the answer either. Often the bitch, once spayed, will put on weight easily (resulting in obesity), become sedentary, and, with the change in hormones, the coat can become excessively long and woolly, as opposed to glossy and silky.

Personally, we are not in favour of spaying or neutering, which, sadly, some veterinary surgeons seem to recommend, often quoting the dangers of pyometra (a life-threatening condition) in bitches, or preventing over-sexual males! Our experience has shown little justification for neutering, providing, of course, the dogs and bitches are not left roaming the streets. Of course, if there is some medical reason for neutering, then it is necessary, but otherwise we prefer to let nature take its course.

DOGS

Males bring no such problems with them, and in the event that you choose/need to have your dog castrated, the process is less invasive.

BUYING A CAVALIER

When you are ready to buy your Cavalier, do not be in too much of a rush. Do your homework and make sure you buy from a reputable breeder. When you have located a breeder, do not expect a puppy to be available immediately. You may have to wait for several months for a puppy from a reputable breeder – it is well worth waiting to buy a typical, quality puppy than rushing to buy from an unknown source.

VISIT A DOG SHOW

Visit a local breed show and see Cavaliers as young as six months and as old as 11 years being

shown. Get a feel for the different ages the Cavalier will go through. This is also another way in which you can contact local breeders. If you like the look of their dogs, and if the dogs appear to be happy and healthy, then talk to the owners about the chances of acquiring a puppy from them. Be prepared to wait for the right puppy; remember, they will be an extension of your family for a significant period of time.

ASK A VET

Call at a local veterinary practice and ask if there is a breeder of Cavaliers whom they would recommend. Arrange to go and see their dogs. Reputable

If you go to a dog show, you will get the opportunity to look at different types of Cavaliers, as well as seeing the different colours.

THE DANGER OF PUPPY FARMS

Avoid the puppy farm at all costs. This is an establishment that breeds for the commercial market, often keeping several popular breeds and producing lots of litters each year. Even worse, some establishments buy puppies in at six weeks of age and sell them on. These kennels often advertise in regional and national newspapers, and breed without concern for breed type or health issues, and the puppies are often poorly reared.

In recent times there has been a growing trend of puppies being bought over the internet. This is fraught with problems, and in a few cases that we are aware of, the breeder has refused to give the money back or indeed take the puppy back when problems have arisen, such as a child becoming allergic when the puppy had been in his new home for less than a week. Many who buy from such sources live to regret it. There are often problems with untypical specimens of the breed, health issues, and irregularities with pedigrees.

We have seen Cavalier puppies from such establishments who were the result of very close inbreeding, and where no health certificates for the dam and sire were available, or, indeed, confirmation that any checks had been carried out for known health problems in the breed.

Health checks are no guarantee, but at least they are an indication that the breeder in question has had the welfare of the animals at heart and is following best practice. We have seen Cavaliers the size of Welsh Springer Spaniels, weedy, undernourished snipey-faced specimens and those that bear little resemblance to a Cavalier at all. So the moral in buying your puppy is: "Buy in haste: repent at leisure".

The puppies should be housed in clean, hygienic accommodation.

Puppies that have been reared in a home environment will already be used to the comings and goings of a busy household.

breeders are always happy and quite proud to show off their canine family.

QUESTIONS TO ASK

Before you even arrange to visit a breeder, there are a number of questions to ask:
- Has the stock, especially the parents of your prospective puppy, been checked for heart murmurs? Do they have current clear heart and eye certificates (i.e. within the last 12 months)?
- How many puppies are in the litter and what colour are they? The average size of a Cavalier litter is around four puppies. The number in a litter will have a bearing on the puppy's

socialisation – a singleton will obviously have missed out on this.
- Was the puppy delivered normally or by Caesarean? Puppies born by Caesarean may be a little smaller but maybe a little more social, as they would have had more handling and maybe some hand rearing. Also, if you are looking for a bitch to breed from in the future, ideally you would be looking to buy your bitch from a litter that was whelped naturally.
- Have the puppies been wormed? Find out how often, with what product, and enquire when they will need worming again.

- Are the puppies Kennel Club registered? If not, there is no guarantee as to the parentage – so why waste your money?
- What age will the puppies be allowed to go to their new homes?
- Will you be allowed to see the dam and littermates?
- How many meals are the puppies being fed a day? What type of food are they getting?
- Have the puppies been vaccinated? Many breeders sell their puppies before inoculations, so you will need to arrange to take your puppy to the vet within 24-48 hours of having brought him home for a full examination. At this stage, you can also discuss a

vaccination policy. We choose never to let a puppy go to his new home until he has been fully vaccinated. We believe you can never be too cautious when it comes to the well-being of the puppy.

• Have the puppies been microchipped? A number of breeders will include this in the puppy's price.

VIEWING THE LITTER

When you visit the breeder of your choice, don't worry if today's dusting hasn't been done, but do make sure that you like the dogs' set-up. Are they used to the vacuum cleaner, the dishwasher and the comings and goings of a busy household, or have they been reared in isolation? Have the puppies been reared in a clean and hygienic environment?

All puppies look adorable – even the less typical examples – so how do you make an assessment? The best plan is to look to the dam of the puppies and, ideally, related siblings for type. If the sire isn't present, ask to see a photograph of him. You should be happy with the appearance of the dogs; they should look typical, pretty Cavaliers and have irreproachable temperaments, being happy, confident and outgoing. Aggression is, thankfully, almost unheard of in the breed. Any signs of timidity should also be avoided. But remember that they are puppies and you are not known to them. However, if you are in any doubt, don't buy the puppy. Nervous dogs are no fun to live with – and you are looking for a companion to share your life for a long time to come.

Do not let your children go dashing about, trying to pick up puppies. Ask the breeder if you may hold or stroke a puppy, and stay seated. Puppies can be very wriggly and before you know it they can have jumped out of your arms. Ideally, sit on the floor – less distance for a puppy to fall if he jumps.

Puppies sleep a lot, so try to visit at a time when they are likely to be lively.

Make sure you see the mother with her puppies to give you an idea of the temperament they are likely to inherit.

ASSESSING THE PUPS

Watching a litter playing is a scene of great joy, especially when they are well reared and healthy. Glossy coats, bright eyes (clear of discharge), well-covered bodies, and wagging tails are all signs of health and wellbeing.

Avoid the thin puppy with a dull, dry coat; the pot-bellied but ribby pup; the very lightly boned pup; the snipey foreface. Above all, avoid nervous puppies who stay at the back of the whelping box or puppy pen. Pups should be bold and come to you.

It is important to tell the breeder what you are looking for: a companion, a show dog, or possibly one for breeding.

COMPANION

My advice is that Cavaliers make great companions and are generally in good health. You can expect a lifespan of 10 to 14 years. Many I have owned have never had to see a vet, except for puppy and booster vaccinations. Of course, all breeds – like all humans – have health problems, but on the whole the Cavalier is a sound, outgoing companion, and I am happy to promote the breed in that light.

If all the correct health indications are there, then choosing a puppy is a matter of personal choice, depending on preference for gender. You might be influenced by colour, markings or facial expression, or by a particularly playful character – or you might find that your puppy chooses you – and how can you say no?

SHOW DOG

If you want a good-quality show puppy, he may be a little more difficult to find and you may need to be prepared to wait for the right prospect. Once you have chosen a line that you admire, be patient. You may have a long wait; really good show prospects are few and far between. Tell the breeder you are prepared to wait for the right puppy.

Reputable breeders never sell puppies as show dogs, because there is no guarantee – we are

The breeder will have spent many hours 'puppy watching' and will be able to guide you with your choice.

dealing with livestock not white goods. The best you can hope for is show potential. Yes, you can look at a puppy and see if he has good breed type – type being a word used to describe breed points. But as Cavaliers are slow to develop, choosing a show-quality pup that is guaranteed to make it in the ring is absolutely impossible. However, there are some pointers that are worth noting.

- **Markings:** On Blenheims and tricolours, the markings should be even on the head and face. An odd face marking can put some judges off, so the first thing I would look for is a well-marked puppy. Sometimes a puppy will get a 'teddy bear coat'; this will be cast at around the teething stage (at around three to four months). The markings on tricolours should also be well broken, with plenty of rich tan above the eyes, under the cheeks, under the tail and on the legs. Rubies and black and tans are 'whole colours', so white patches would be classed as a fault.
- **Temperament:** Never choose a puppy that does not come to you, as he will never have the confidence that is required in the ring. Temperaments can alter in Cavaliers, so my advice is to be guided by the breeder.
- **Conformation:** Is the puppy sound on the move? I would be looking for a proud head carriage, good topline, and good bone. I do not want to see a puppy at 10 weeks with big, knuckly bone, particularly round the front legs. This would indicate to me a lot more growth.

Often, you will find a small bump at the top of the nose; this indicates length to come on the nose. The Breed Standard asks for a 1.5-inch stop (3.8 cms). The stop is from the forehead to the tip of the nose. You will also need to check if a puppy has got a correct bite – i.e. a scissor bite where the teeth on the upper jaw closely overlap the teeth on the lower jaw.

CHOOSING A SHOW PUPPY

The breeder will help you to assess show potential.

This is a high-quality puppy, and is a very good example of breed type.

THE WAITING GAME

If, like me, you choose to show, I have no doubt you will make many friends and acquaintances, and, with the right attitude, have an absorbing hobby and enjoy a great deal of satisfaction. After 36 years plus of showing these charming little spaniels, my enthusiasm is still as great. Such loyal spaniels deserve our trust, love, and loyalty – after all, they give us so much and ask for so little.

When my partner and I decided that we wanted to enter into the world of showing dogs, having at that time acquired Cavaliers, I have to say they were great ambassadors for the breed and we loved them dearly, but they were not show stoppers. After what seemed like a lifetime – almost two years – we took possession of our foundation bitch, who lies behind all our kennel stock. The wait was worthwhile, having subsequently made up 19 Blenheim Champions, and, at the time of writing, we have the privilege of owning the breed record holder. So that two-year wait was more than worthwhile.

Ch. Ricksbury Royal Temptress (Nellie): Bitch breed record holder.
Photo courtesy: Russell Fine Art.

Taking on an older dog can be very rewarding.

- **Expression:** Does the puppy have an appealing expression? Yes, all puppies look cute, but I am looking for a good eye set, dark in colour, and soft and gentle in expression, with eyes set well apart.

You can see that it is not easy to pick a show puppy at 10 weeks. But if you have gone to a reputable breeder, and the puppy ticks most of the boxes I have mentioned, you should be OK. I would emphasise to anyone who would want to show to be patient, and to be prepared to wait for the right puppy.

AN OLDER CAVALIER

While the thought of seeing a puppy grow up appeals to many, some prefer to take on an adult. An older dog will be more sedate and will have gone past the demands of frequent puppy meals; he may be used to the lead, as well as being house trained and car trained.

Often, retired or older people find the older Cavalier more manageable. How might you discover these? Occasionally, breeders might have an older Cavalier available, perhaps one of a year old, who has been retained as a show prospect but who has not quite fulfilled his

early potential. Or there is the retired show dog, who might have had a good career in the show ring, perhaps has had a litter or two, but now would enjoy the comforts of living as a house pet, rather than as part of a bigger Cavalier family. Breeders have had great happiness from seeing some of their mature show dogs settle in as loved house pets. Their initial anguish and worry about letting a dog go has been quickly dispersed when hearing from the new owners about how quickly the dog has settled into his new lifestyle.

If you are taking on an older Cavalier, you might be prepared

The Cavalier is surprisingly adaptable and he will not take long to settle into a new home.

for a trial period of a couple of weeks to a month, to see that the dog has settled in. He might need a little house training as he gets used to your routine and set-up, or he may have been a kennel dog that has to learn new ways – but, in most cases, things go quite smoothly.

When breeders part with older stock, you should expect to pay a reduced price on the puppy price – with the breeders sometimes withholding the pedigree as a guarantee that the dog is not to be used for breeding and is simply a house pet.

RESCUE SCHEMES

Another source of adult Cavaliers is the breed club rescue scheme. Many Cavalier breed clubs run schemes for rehoming Cavaliers who, for a variety of reasons, have ended up in the scheme, perhaps due to bereavement, a family break-up, or as a result of a hasty acquisition without thinking of the required degree of commitment. These Cavaliers might range from young dogs to veterans, with most generally aged six years and over.

As a prospective adopter, you will be carefully scrutinised, and you may have to wait until the right Cavalier comes along. Again, a trial period in your house is customary. It may take an older rescued dog a while to adjust to a new home, but this is a very rewarding situation for both sides, when things work out.

THE NEW ARRIVAL

Chapter 4

So, you have decided on the Cavalier King Charles Spaniel as your chosen breed of dog. You have done your research, found a reputable breeder and chosen your puppy. Or you may have decided to take on an adult, either through a rescue organisation or one that a breeder has decided to rehome. Either way, what preparations do you need to make for your new arrival?

Firstly, where in your house would be the most suitable place to locate your puppy's bed or crate? Most people opt for the kitchen, as this is usually the hub of the household and where the family will spend most of their time – a Cavalier, in particular, loves nothing more than just being with his people. A good point, too, is that most kitchen floors are tiled or laid with lino, which is hardwearing and easy to

clean should the need arise. If your kitchen has a door out into the garden, this will come in most handy when toilet training your puppy.

When you have decided on the best place for your dog, check that there aren't any sharp edges to cupboards or doors, and that there aren't any valuable pieces of furniture that could be chewed. Also check that there are no interesting wires lying around within easy reach that may prove irresistible.

Then look to see if you have a cosy little corner, or just a suitable space, where a crate or bed would fit nicely. It doesn't take long for a dog to recognise his own little spot.

SAFETY IN THE GARDEN

Next, you must be sure that your garden is absolutely 'dog proof'. Cavaliers have an amazing knack of finding the tiniest hole or gap

in a fence to wriggle through. Go around the boundaries of your garden, checking every nook and cranny, particularly under large shrubs or trees. If your garden has wooden fencing, check that there are no gaps between the fence and ground that could easily be dug into.

The best way of securing any areas of doubt is with fine weld mesh that can be purchased from any good garden centre. This can then be tacked on to existing fencing, and, if needs be, slightly dug into the ground. I would recommend using weld mesh in preference to chicken wire, as it is far more durable and is easy to cut without leaving any sharp, uneven edges that could poke into eyes.

Look at the plants in your garden, too. Some plants are highly toxic to dogs – such as laburnum trees, hydrangea and foxglove – so you may need to

Cavaliers are great explorers, so make sure your house and garden are free from potential hazards.

take steps to ensure that your new puppy does not have easy access to such things.

OTHER CONSIDERATIONS

Do you have steps in your garden or going out of your house? These can prove hazardous for your puppy if he runs around and takes a flying leap! If he happens to misjudge the distance, he could easily end up with a broken leg or worse. The same caution should be observed if you have any low walls in your garden – could the puppy jump off this wall and hurt himself?

Is there a pond in your garden? Most dogs are natural swimmers, but a pond can be a potential death-trap for a pup. It may not be so much that the puppy cannot swim, but if he should fall in without your knowledge, he may exhaust himself and drown while struggling to get out. I have heard of this happening too many times, and it is devastating for all those involved. A temporary cover or fencing around the pond would be sufficient until the puppy is fully grown.

Do you have a side path from the front to the back of your house? Is there a gate there? Is it secure? Is there a gap underneath that a dog could squeeze through? These are all things that you must take into account before you collect your new puppy, as it is always better to take preventative measures than to have to live with the consequences.

BUYING EQUIPMENT

A Cavalier does not need a vast amount of equipment, but there are a few essentials for the shopping list:

CRATES

To my mind, the most important piece of equipment for a new puppy is a crate or 'indoor kennel'. This should measure approximately 24 ins long, 19 ins high, and 21 ins wide (61 x 48 x 53 cms) – the ideal size for an adult Cavalier. There are many types of crates available on the market these days – metal, fabric and plastic, those with single doors, two doors and, in some cases, three doors. Prices vary to a huge degree, but the average price you would expect to pay for a good-quality crate is about £40.

I would recommend a crate with two doors, one at the front and one at the side; this gives you the option of putting the crate in the most suitable place for you while still having easy access. A lot of people find the idea of crating their dog distasteful, but rest assured, the dog won't mind it half as much as you will. Imagine this scenario: your children have some of their friends round – it a nice sunny day and they are running in and out, leaving doors open. Where is the puppy? Oh yes, he is safe and secure in his crate.

We have had no end of people who have bought puppies from us, and who, initially, baulked at the idea of a crate when we first suggested it to them. So we lent them a crate with their new puppy for a few weeks, and they all, without exception, have come back and bought one from us. We have also found that if you go away and take your dog with you, many hoteliers or property owners are more willing to accept a dog, knowing that he can be confined to a cage if left, rather than running amok in a hotel bedroom. This is where the fabric crates are particularly useful, as they are lighter to move around with you, although you may find a particularly determined dog may be able to break out of one. I also wouldn't recommend one for young puppies, as they may chew it.

BEDDING

There are many different types of bedding available. The most practical bedding to use is a product called Vetbed. This has a fleece/woollen top with an

If you accustom your puppy to his crate from an early stage, he will soon settle in his doggy den.

absorbent underside. It can be purchased from your vet or any good pet shop. The beauty of this product, especially for puppies, is that if the pup has an 'accident', the urine will soak straight through to the underside, leaving the top completely dry. It is also fully washable and will last for a long time.

You can also buy 'doggy duvets', which are quilts, usually with a removable, fully washable cover. These are very cosy and

nice for the puppy to snuggle into. The only downside with these is that if the duvet isn't fully stitched in, it can all bunch up in the middle after it is washed and become pretty useless.

As to the type of bed you choose for your Cavalier, the range is vast. There are beanbags, wicker baskets and plastic beds. Any of these would be fine, but bear in mind, especially with a young puppy, the 'chewability'

factor of any item.
Wicker baskets,
for example, seem
to be a particular
favourite. In quite
a short space of
time, a wicker
basket can end up
in a real mess,
leaving sharp
pieces of wicker
sticking out – a
potential hazard
to eyes. Dogs also
love beanbags,
but again, any
amount of
chewing over time
could result in
the beans spilling
out and, apart
from the
inconvenience of
having thousands
of tiny
polystyrene balls
all over the place, they can be
dangerous if swallowed in any
quantity. A plastic bed with a
cosy piece of Vetbed would
probably be the most practical
equipment to buy, as they are
both long-lasting and easy to
clean.

FOOD AND WATER BOWLS
Food and water bowls range from
pretty ceramic bowls decorated
with patterns, brightly coloured
plastic bowls in a variety of
shapes and sizes, to bowls made
of heavy-duty stainless steel. The
ceramic bowls may look
attractive, but they are easily
broken and it only needs an over-
excited dog to crash the bowl

There is a wide variety of different collars and leads to choose from.

against something while he is
eating. The plastic bowls are
probably the cheapest to buy,
but they are far from
indestructible and chewed edges
soon become very dirty and can
harbour bacteria.

I would recommend a couple
of stainless steel bowls: one for
the food and one for water. It is
useful to note that you can buy
'spaniel' bowls in this material.
These are bowls that look almost
like an upside-down funnel, in
that they are tall, and narrower at
the top than they are at the
bottom. These bowls are
particularly good for Cavaliers, as
their unique shape stops the
dog's ears hanging in the bowl
and getting wet or coated in

food. Metal bowls
are also the most
hygienic; they are
easy to clean and
can even be put in
a dishwasher.

If you have a
crate in which you
feed and sleep
your dog, you can
also buy special
metal bowls that
clip on to the crate
side, therefore
allowing your dog
access to water at
all times. These are
known as 'coop
cups' and are
usually sold for
birdcages, but, in
the right size, work
just as well for
dogs.

COLLARS AND LEADS
Collars and leads are available in
various materials and designs.
Whichever material you opt for,
be sure to get one that is
completely secure and fits
properly.

The proper fit of a collar
should be that the collar goes
round the dog's neck
comfortably with enough leeway
either to tighten or loosen
should the dog's neck size
change with either weight gain or
loss. When done up, you should
be able to insert two fingers
comfortably between the collar
and the dog's neck – without
being able to pull the collar over
the dog's head.

Leather collars usually have a

buckle fit. These are probably the strongest, but they can wear and break where the holes are punched, so check them regularly for signs of damage.

There are lots of 'novelty' leather collars available, too, with studded decorations in various colours – gold, silver or jewels – and the name of your dog can even be spelt out in diamante along the collar.

Nylon fabric collars usually come with two types of fastening: a buckle fastening or a push-in clip fastening. Many material collars are also 'one size fits all', where there are no permanent holes punched along the length, but where the spike can be pushed through at any place to fit. These are useful for a growing puppy, as they are lightweight and easily adjustable, but you can be left with a great long piece hanging untidily down, which can wear and fray.

The push-in clip fastening collars are a piece of nylon fabric with two plastic end pieces that can be pushed or clipped into each other and lock.

These collars are also easily adjustable, and they come in a myriad of colours, patterns and designs. I personally recommend this type of collar to my new puppy owners. They are tough and durable, and much easier to put on and take off. The fastening is also a better safety feature, as it can be quickly released should the collar get caught on something around the home or while out walking. It doesn't take much for a puppy to panic and

Novelty gear is fun as long as you have practical options for everyday use.

end up twisting the collar even tighter, risking strangulation.

The main decisions needed when buying a lead are length and comfort. I wouldn't advise the use of a metal lead for the main reason that the simple act of walking your dog would cause the lead, because of the weight of the chain, to sway backward and forward and subsequently hit the dog in the face. They are more suitable to big dogs.

The length of the lead should be enough to give you some slack when the dog is walking to heel but not so long as to trip you or

the dog up, or that you have a great wodge rolled into your hand to restrain the dog closely. The ideal length for a Cavalier is about 40" (1 metre). Most leads will have a metal clip fastening on the end, which is by far the safest, but do check for wear and tear as, over the years, the clip may become loose and it is not unheard for them to spring open and break.

Another alternative is a nylon fabric slip lead, which is a collar and lead all in one. These come in two varieties: a collar attached to a lead with a piece of chain, or a length of fabric with a ring on the end. The fabric is threaded back on itself to form a circle, which is placed around the dog's neck. This is quite useful to keep in your pocket while out walking, just in case of an emergency.

GROOMING EQUIPMENT

With his long, silky coat a Cavalier requires a certain amount of grooming – usually, once a week is sufficient. The main equipment you will need to buy is:

- **Slicker brush:** This is basically a rubber pad, which has lots of little wire hooks on it. This brush is ideal for using on the dog's long feathering, as it will gently tease out any knots or snags. It can also be used on the short body coat to release and remove any dead hair. Caution must be paid when using this, however, as if it is used too vigorously on some parts of the body, it can cause a rash on the skin.
- **Medium-toothed comb:** The most practical comb to buy is a wooden or plastic-handled comb with medium to fine teeth. This should be used after the slicker brush to ensure any awkward places, such as the armpits or the inside of the back legs, are free from knots and tangles. It will also remove any dead hair missed by the slicker.
- **Bristle brush:** This is useful as an everyday brush. It stimulates the blood under the surface of the skin and helps to improve the condition and shine of the coat.
- **Nail clippers:** I would recommend buying guillotine nail clippers. They are by far the easiest to use and are the most comfortable for the dog. They also have a built-in safety feature to guard against cutting the nail too short and causing it to bleed.
- **Tooth care:** There are products available, either from your vet or over the counter, to keep a dog's teeth healthy. There are special doggy toothpastes and brushes, bones and chews, which can be used to help combat tooth disease.
- For information on grooming, see Chapter Five: The Best of Care.

Stock up on grooming gear, as your puppy will need to get used to being groomed from an early age.

TOYS

A Cavalier is a game little dog and will spend hours playing on his own or with company. He will enjoy any kind of toy, including plastic squeaky 'hotdogs', rope tuggers, rubber balls, or even an old sock with a knot tied in the middle. Make sure toys are completely safe, as accidents can happen all too easily when a piece of a toy, such as a squeaker, is swallowed.

BONES

If you need to leave your puppy for any length of time, a sterilised white bone will keep him occupied. They are virtually indestructible and will provide hours of chewing. Another good option is sterilised cow hooves. I wouldn't recommend rawhide chews. Although very popular with our dogs, we have had experiences of them getting very soggy when wet, and they can get stuck around a dog's teeth or, even more worrying, down the throat.

ID

By law, a dog must wear, at all times, a collar with an identity disc, showing the owner's address and telephone number. Some owners also choose to put the dog's name on the disc and their vet's telephone number. In this day and age, with dog theft being quite big business, it is advisable also to get your dog permanently identified. There are two ways of doing this, either with a microchip or tattoo. Each method is backed up by a nationwide database where all contact details are recorded.

MICROCHIPPING

Most vets will be happy to microchip your pet and register the details, or there are various organisations, such as the RSPCA, PDSA or Dogs Trust, that also offer this service. The chip is the size of a grain of rice and is inserted into the skin, usually just between the shoulderblades of the dog, with a special needle. Each chip has its own unique number, which can only be read with a special scanner to identify the dog and match it to the

Cavalier puppies are very playful, and will enjoy a homemade toy just as much as anything you can buy in the shops – as long as it is 100 per cent safe.

owner details recorded at the time of implantation.

TATTOOING

Some breeders choose to tattoo their puppies before they go to their new homes. This is, again, a simple procedure, which is done at approximately six weeks of age. It is a permanent identification number that is stamped inside the ear, then sprayed with permanent ink, and expands so it is easily readable as the puppy grows. Older dogs can also be tattooed in a virtually painless procedure that requires neither anaesthetic nor sedation. This number, and all your and your dog's details are then registered with the National Dog Tattoo Register.

FINDING A VET

If you are buying your puppy from a local breeder, it is a good idea to use their vet. The breeder may well have had the litter health-checked, so the vet will already have all the puppies' details. Most reputable breeders, once they find a good vet, will stick with them through thick and thin. To me this is as good a recommendation as any. If, however, you are travelling a distance to collect your puppy, and you are a first-time owner, you will need to find another source. But bear in mind that it doesn't always follow that a vet who suits one person will necessarily suit you. It's like your own doctor: you need to find someone you can trust.

Look through your local telephone directory. Make a few phone calls. Go and visit the practices. See what set-up they have. A lot of veterinary practises have fabulous facilities, incorporating a hospital and a laboratory, and some have vets who specialise in certain areas, such as cardiology, orthopaedics or ophthalmology.

Try to meet some of the staff and see how they come across. There is a lot to be said for first impressions, and if the front desk or reception staff are friendly and informative, the chances are that their bosses will be the same.

At last the big day arrives and it is time to collect your puppy.

COLLECTING YOUR PUPPY

So the day has arrived to collect your new Cavalier. It is advisable that you take someone with you when you go, especially if you are buying a puppy. This will make the return journey easier, as your helper will be able to hold the puppy while you are concentrating on the driving. I would always recommend collecting in the morning, as this will then give the puppy the rest of the day to explore his new surroundings and settle in.

When you collect your puppy you should be given five items of paperwork:

- A pedigree for the puppy
- A diet sheet
- A receipt/contract of sale
- A bill/certificate of health and worming certificate
- A vaccination card, if applicable.

PEDIGREE

The pedigree is a document that should show at least four generations of the puppy's breeding: from the sire and dam, through to the great-great grandparents etc, and should be signed, by the breeder, to certify that it is correct to the 'best of their knowledge'.

DIET SHEET

The diet sheet should clearly set out exactly what the puppy has been eating, amounts he is given per meal, and also how many times he is fed during the day. It should also give pointers on how you should progress with the puppy's feeding regime – i.e. when to increase the amounts of food, when to drop a meal, etc.

RECEIPT/CONTRACT OF SALE

The receipt will acknowledge the transaction of the monies that change hands between you and the breeder, and any terms and conditions that the breeder stipulates for the sale of this dog. For example, "That the puppy is not to be bred from or shown" or "In the event you are unable to keep the puppy, it is to be returned to the breeder and not sold on."

It may also stipulate that endorsements have been placed upon this puppy with the Kennel Club and only the breeder can remove these. There are two endorsements that can be used:

- Progeny not Eligible for Registration: This means that if the puppy produces puppies of its own, either as a sire or a dam, the said puppies cannot be registered with the English Kennel Club.
- Not Eligible for the Issue of an Export Pedigree: This means that the puppy, if sent abroad,

cannot be registered with the country of destination's affiliated kennel club, and therefore cannot be shown or bred from in that country.

This is merely a way that reputable breeders may choose to protect their breeding lines and any puppies they sell. Most breeders will require a signature from you to show that you agree to buy the puppy under the terms and conditions laid out.

BILL/CERTIFICATE OF HEALTH

Some breeders may go to the trouble and expense of having the puppies checked by a vet prior to them going to their new homes. This is useful to new owners, as it provides peace of mind that the puppy you are buying has been given a clean bill of health. It may also make note of any slight anomalies, such as umbilical hernias or ear mites, which may need to be monitored or treated.

Many people expect, at the time of sale, to be given the Kennel Club registration certificate for their puppy, but sometimes a breeder may not have registered the puppies. This should give no cause for alarm. The Kennel Club allows 12 months to register a litter of puppies from the date of birth, and if the breeder is keeping a puppy from the litter themselves, they may wish to wait a while before they decide on a name for their puppy. As long as you have written confirmation that the puppy will be registered in due course, that should suffice.

Some breeder will have their puppies health-checked before they go to their new homes.

The breeder should also give you information on any worming treatments that your puppy has had, and advise you as to when they will need another treatment. It is of great importance to know this information, so you can work out a worming regime for the future. By the time you collect your new puppy, at the age of approximately eight weeks, he should have been wormed at least twice. There are many products for worming on the market and the breeder should advise which is the best to use. Personally, I recommend

FEEDING ADVICE

Many people don't realise just how traumatic it is to change homes. Often, a dog will not eat for the first day or two. This is nothing to worry about! Offer your puppy or older dog his meal at the time laid out in the diet sheet, and then leave it for 15 minutes. Ideally, shut your Cavalier in his crate with his food bowl. If he hasn't eaten anything in that time frame, simply take the food away until the next allotted mealtime. A puppy or adult can go without food for at least 24 hours without any harm coming to them.

Do not start hand feeding. This is simply the worst thing you can do. A Cavalier is very canny and will quickly cotton on to the fact that if he doesn't eat of his own accord, you will feed him. Hand feeding not only takes a lot of time and patience on your part, but it creates a very fussy dog.

If your Cavalier doesn't eat his food readily, do not change it or add a little bribe. Changing the diet, or adding something that the puppy has not eaten before, is the quickest way to give him an upset tummy and diarrhoea. Added to the stress of changing homes, a runny tummy will quickly pull a puppy down and can make them quite ill.

Most healthy, happy puppies will eat their diet voraciously. It may take a few days for the puppy to start clearing his bowl, but all will be well if you stand firm.

If, for whatever reason, you decide after a while that you wish to change the diet, it must be done very gradually over a few days. Slowly introduce some of the new food, a tiny amount at a time, into each meal, while at the same time cutting down slightly on the old food. Do this each time, gradually increasing the amount of new food per meal until you have completely cut out the old. Again, changing the diet too quickly at any age can cause an upset tummy.

products that are only available from your vet. For more information, see Chapter Eight: Happy and Healthy.

VACCINATION CARD

Some, but not all, breeders may have had a puppy vaccinated prior to collection. If so, you should be given a card showing details of which vaccination has been given, on what date and when the next shot is due.

COLLECTING AN ADULT

Whether your new Cavalier is coming through rescue or from a breeder, you will need similar back up and information.

In the case of a rescue dog, the chances are you won't receive a pedigree or any Kennel Club papers, but the society involved should be able to give you details about the dog's diet and his vaccination and worming history. The dog will probably have been checked by a vet, so you will be able to find out about any health problems.

If you are buying an older dog from a breeder – for example, a bitch that they no longer wish to breed from – you also may not get any Kennel Club papers, but you should be given the pedigree

and diet sheet, records of worming and vaccinations, and a receipt. Again, the breeder will probably have had the dog checked for problems.

MEETING THE HUMAN FAMILY

If you have children, it is likely they will want to invite all their friends round to view the new baby. I would advise that this is left for a couple of days, to let your puppy get his bearings and settle. Don't allow too many children at a time – four would be a maximum.

When there are a lot of

If you are taking on an older dog, find out as much information as you can about his health record and his feeding regime.

children around a new puppy, it is important to keep a calm, quiet atmosphere. Noisy children jumping around, will, at best, unsettle a puppy and, at worse, frighten him. Make sure that children play with the puppy while they are sitting on the floor and not carrying the pup around. It is just too easy for a puppy to jump or fall from a child's arms and be seriously injured.

MEETING THE ANIMAL FAMILY
When introducing a newcomer to other animals in your household, the best thing to do is to take

your time. A boisterous, inquisitive puppy may not go down well with the resident dog or cat. Let them meet on their terms and in their own time. An older dog may growl at the new arrival to begin with. Don't chastise him: this is his way of setting out the boundaries and laying down a few house rules – most puppies will accept this. It won't be long before you find them playing or snuggled up asleep together.

Many cats will turn tail and run from the intruder but will eventually accept the youngster, usually with a very long-suffering

attitude! Just keep an eye that the cat doesn't swipe the puppy with his sharp claws.

THE FIRST NIGHT AND BEYOND
After a long, busy day, your puppy will be ready for bed. Again, this is where a crate is invaluable. Imagine what it must be like for a puppy to be taken from all his littermates, to a strange house, and left on his own in a large dark room. It is when puppies are frightened or bored like this that they can become noisy and/or destructive. So, you have bought your crate

and put it in a suitable place – now all you need to do is make it cosy and snug. It is a good idea to cover the crate with a big blanket. This will keep out any drafts and also make it feel like a little den. Put a layer of newspaper on the floor of the crate, and position the Vetbed at one end. Hang the coop cup on the side, remembering to put it low enough for the puppy to reach.

A soft toy is also a good idea, as this provides something for the puppy to nestle against and to play with if needed. Give a couple of biscuits, say 'Goodnight' and turn out the light. It is highly likely that your puppy will yap and cry. This will usually go on for, at the most, half an hour. Once the puppy has realised that all his efforts are in vain, he will give up and go to sleep. Whatever you do, don't give in. As with feeding, the puppy will soon learn how to get your attention.

HOUSE TRAINING

The basic rules to remember are that your puppy is very much like a baby: he sleeps, eats and plays. A puppy will need to toilet as soon as he wakes and after each meal. At these times, pop the puppy out in the garden. Go with him and encourage him to do what you require, using a simple command (such as "Toilet" or "Wee-wee"). Then, when the puppy has performed, lavish him with praise and take him back inside.

Anytime you see the puppy sniffing around in an urgent kind of way, which usually signifies a motion, quickly pop him outside and encourage him as before. After a few times of doing this,

Take your puppy out to the garden at regular intervals and he will soon understand what is required.

Settling into a new home is a tiring business, so make sure your puppy has the opportunity to rest.

you can put the puppy out alone and encourage from the other side of the door. Your puppy will soon learn what is to be done, and, before long, he will ask to go out.

SETTLING IN

It is important that your Cavalier understands the house rules from an early age. If you do not wish your puppy to go on the furniture, make sure he knows this from day one. Cavaliers are so willing to please and are easily taught.

You will also need to accustom your puppy to being handled all over. Look in his mouth, go over his body, and touch and hold his feet. All of this will be useful training to get him used to being groomed, or examined by a vet.

In those first few weeks, there is a lot of hard work involved in making a Cavalier part of your family, but if you follow the simple directions that have been outlined, your new Cavalier will soon be a treasured member of your family.

THE BEST OF CARE

5
Chapter

The dietary needs of a Cavalier King Charles Spaniel need to be given very careful consideration. Planning for a dog's wellbeing begins before birth, continues with the breeder at weaning time, and ultimately becomes your responsibility for his lifetime. General wellbeing comes from within, and what you put in will show on the outside in your Cavalier's coat and condition

Whichever diet you choose, ultimately your dog requires a balance of the following nutrients:

- **Protein:** To provide essential amino acids, which are necessary for growth in puppies, maintenance of adults, and a healthy immune system. Protein can be found in fresh beef, lamb, chicken, turkey, fish and eggs, and are

also good natural sources of the B group vitamins: B1, B2, B3, B6 and B12. Omega 3 can be obtained through oily fish, such as pilchards, sardines and herrings (if using tinned fish, only use fish based in oil), and spinach.
- **Carbohydrates:** For energy, and rich in fibre. Comes in the form of wholewheat grains, rice, and pasta.
- **Vitamins and minerals:** Zinc, iron, and magnesium are essential to support a healthy immune system. Dark green, leafy vegetables are a natural source of iron, B vitamins and folic acid. Calcium is needed for strong bones and teeth. A natural source of calcium can be obtained through eggs, fish, and dark green, leafy vegetables. A word of caution here, as the over-supplementation of calcium can lead to bone deformities in

puppies. If your Cavalier is healthy and having a well-balanced diet, extra supplementation should not be considered without veterinary advice.

THE RIGHT START
A reputable and conscientious breeder will have spent many years perfecting the diet that suits their puppies and will have researched many of the popular and not so popular diets. It is therefore well worth following their diet plan, unless there is a specific need to make a change.

Most breeders will supply you with enough food for a few days, so you will be able to continue feeding your puppy the same food he has been used to. This will help ease the transition into his new home, which is a traumatic time. The puppy is learning to cope with new surroundings, and changing his

You need to feed a well-balanced diet that caters for all your dog's nutritional needs.

diet at this time could cause unnecessary upset. The breeder will also provide you with a diet sheet so you can follow the same feeding regime as to the number of meals and the amount to feed.

CHOOSING A DIET

Choosing the right diet can be a minefield, as there are so many choices and considerations. Basically, the aim is to find a diet that suits your dog, you and your purse. This is a personal choice, but it is one of the most important choices you will make for your Cavalier throughout his lifetime.

If a diet has suited your puppy from weaning, then is there really a need to change it? The old saying of "If it isn't broken, don't try fixing it" is very true. However, you may have your own theories on nutrition or you may have concerns about your Cavalier's health. In all cases, it is important to be aware of the different types of diet, as your Cavalier's needs may change at some time during his life.

HOMEMADE

Some prefer to feed a homemade diet with fresh meat, as they feel that they have total control over the ingredients fed and vitamins needed to suit each individual dog. It is, however, important to make sure you feed a balanced diet that fulfils all nutritional requirements.

THE BARF DIET

The BARF diet (Biologically Appropriate Raw Food – also known as 'Bones and Raw Food') was derived from the theory that dogs in the wild would consume all parts of a carcass, and that by eating the whole body, including the stomach and its contents of grasses and vegetables, the dog received a balanced diet. The vet Dr Ian Billinghurst has written two books – *Give your Dog a Bone* and *Grow your Own Pups with Bones* – which explain this regime in detail. In this context, I can only outline the basic theory.

As a general rule of thumb, the BARF diet should consist of 60 per cent raw meaty bones, and 40 per cent of other food,

HOMEMADE DIET SHEET

BABY PUPPY (eight weeks to three months)

Feed four meals a day, consisting of two meat meals and two milk meals; or substitute one meal with scrambled egg. Gradually increase the amount given according to the puppy's growth. Add some lightly cooked vegetables (green beans, carrots or broccoli) two or three times per week to the meat meals.

- Breakfast: Scrambled egg with either 1/4 slice of brown bread and a little spread (cut into bite-size pieces) or 1 tablespoon of cooked rice or pasta. Alternatively, baby rice mixed with a little warm goat's milk or unsweetened evaporated milk.
- Lunch: 2 oz (57 g) raw minced beef plus 1 tablespoon of puppy mixer. Gradually increase to 3 oz (85 g) and 1 tablespoon of puppy mixer over the next four weeks (i.e. 1/4 oz per week).
- Tea: 2 oz (57 g) cooked chicken or turkey mince, or uncooked minced beef or tripe, plus 1 tablespoon of rice or pasta or puppy meal. Gradually increase to 3 oz (85 g) meat and 2 tablespoons of rice, pasta or puppy mixer.
- Supper: As for breakfast.

PUPPY (four months to six months)

Reduce to three meals a day. This should consist of two meat meals. Scrambled egg can be substituted for one meal two or three times per week.

- Breakfast: Substitute milk meal for meat, increasing the meat over next three months to 4 oz (113 g) meat plus 2 tablespoons of pasta, rice or biscuit. Substitute puppy meal for wholemeal terrier meal (hard biscuit).
- Lunch: Same as breakfast, or one scrambled egg plus 2-3 oz (57-85 g) pasta or rice (still only give a maximum of three eggs per week).
- Supper: Same as breakfast.

JUNIOR (six months to nine months)

Reduce to two meat meals a day, given morning and evening: 6-8 oz (170-227 g) meat plus approximately 0.5 oz (14 g) terrier grade wholemeal biscuit.

ADULT CAVALIER

4-6 oz (113-170 g) meal and approximately 1 oz (28 g) biscuit fed once daily, or this can be split into two small meals if preferred. If your dog looks too fat, then feed slightly less, decreasing the meat by 1/4 oz. If he/she looks on the lean side, increase the diet by 1/4 oz (7 g) weekly until the ideal weight is reached.

Adding a few daily supplements to your dog's diet, such as a little vegetable oil, can help to keep the skin and coat in good condition. Garlic acts as a cleanser and is good for the blood. It also helps to prevent infestation by fleas and worms – however, it can be toxic if fed in large quantities, so don't over-feed.

A puppy will need four meals a day when he first arrives in his new home.

Keep a check on your Cavalier's weight in order to calculate how much food he needs.

including minced beef, tripe, large chunks of turkey or chicken breast, or shin of beef. A Cavalier needs approximately two raw chicken wings or large poultry necks per meal, adding hearts, liver or other offal once a week. Pulped vegetables, and fruit should be fed no more than three times per week. A vitamin and mineral supplement needs to be given on a daily basis.

Dogs love the bones, which help keep their teeth clean, and many that advocate using the BARF diet say that their dogs are healthier. Owners with dogs who suffer from allergies report that the allergies clear much quicker, and, due to firmer, chalkier stools, it helps dogs suffering with blocked anal gland problems, which is often a direct result of feeding soft food. Although a little more effort is needed in the

beginning, this diet soon becomes a familiar way of feeding.

Eggs are an excellent source of protein and provide omega 3 essential fatty acids. Eggs can be fed either cooked or raw, but if fed raw, only use the yolk, as the white contains avidin, which can prevent the absorption of biotin. The biotin in the yolk of an egg helps maintain a healthy coat.

As with any change of feeding regime, a BARF diet must be introduced gradually. Bones should never be fed cooked, as they splinter and can cause considerable damage as they pass through the dog. When making the transition, start giving your Cavalier his first bone after he has eaten his normal food for the day, – with a full stromach he will be less likely to bolt down the bone. Never leave your Cavalier unattended. Puppies should be

started with finely ground bones, only allowing them a large raw bone to chew as they grow bigger and have a strong enough jaw to crunch the bone into bite-sized pieces. Puppies should be supervised at all time when chewing bones.

COMMERCIALLY PREPARED FOOD

There are many commercially prepared dog foods on the market, which come in different forms: dry complete, canned food, pouches, or hermetically sealed in tubs.

COMPLETE FOOD

Complete food is exactly as it suggests: a complete balanced diet. Vitamins, minerals and calcium are already added in the correct amounts, and to add anything else will cause an

A complete diet is manufactured to meet all your dog's nutritional needs.

Canned food is fed with a mixer biscuit.

imbalance in the formula. It is a convenient diet for the busy households of today, and will give your dog the nutrition he needs.

There are different protein levels to suit each stage of your Cavalier's development. The manufacturers suggest that puppies need a higher protein level of approximately 30-33 per cent, containing 20 per cent fats, than an adult who will need 25-27 per cent protein and 14-16 per cent fats. The elderly dog will still require the same protein levels, but should be fed according to his exercise tolerance levels. Obviously, feeding the same amount as an active dog would cause an elderly dog to become grossly overweight.

The guesswork is taken out of making the right choice for your

Cavalier as it develops from puppy to veteran.

CANNED FOOD

Traditional prepared food comes in cans or pouches, and these have easy-to-follow guidelines. This food is usually fed with either a small-bite mixer or terrier meal. The advantages of feeding prepared food is that it is quick and easy for the owner, and the guesswork is taken out of whether you are feeding a balanced diet. The disadvantage of this type of diet is that you have no control over what your Cavalier is eating; you are reliant on the manufacturers getting it right.

All quantities fed are manufacturer's recommendations and these are guidelines only. The RDA (the total daily allowance recommended to keep your dog fit and healthy) for puppies

should be divided into three or four small meals per day, and an adult's RDA should be fed in one or divided into two smaller meals.

Whichever feeding regime you choose, changing your Cavalier's diet needs to be a gradual process over five to seven days; substituting a small amount of the current diet with the new one.

FEEDING METHODS

Once you have chosen a suitable diet for your Cavalier, you need to decide what method of feeding will suit both you and your dog.

REGULAR MEALS

Keeping your Cavalier to regular meal times provides routine. If you are feeding one meal a day, feed at the same time every day;

It is your job to keep your Cavalier lean and healthy.

changing his meal to different times of day will unsettle him and he will be forever looking for his food, never knowing when it will arrive.

If you are feeding twice daily, space the meals well apart by feeding first thing in the morning and again at around tea time, which will allow your dog a chance to relieve himself before bedtime. Never allow your Cavalier to make a nuisance of himself at your mealtimes; he should never be fed food from the table – this is a bad habit and can lead to your Cavalier becoming obese.

FREE FEEDING
Free feeding allows your Cavalier to help himself whenever he feels like it. Food is made available 24 hours a day. As Cavaliers are generally food-orientated, you could find that your dog eats all his food in one go, which would make him very uncomfortable. Gorging would also be bad for his digestive system, and would almost certainly give him a tummy upset. Often free feeders become sluggish and lethargic, and don't have any real gusto for meals.

If you choose this method, it is best to use a complete dry food, as a moist food will go hard after a few hours. In the warmer months this could cause a problem with flies, which may lay eggs on to the food, resulting in all sorts of problems for your Cavalier. Care must be taken when choosing this method. It is not one that is recommended by most vets or breeders.

GROOMING
Nothing is nicer than seeing a well-groomed Cavalier, with his long, silky coat gleaming. The Breed Standard states that the Cavalier should be free from any trimming, although trimming the hair underneath the pad is

THE DANGERS OF OBESITY

Most Cavaliers love their food and will try their utmost to persuade you with those doe eyes to give them everything you eat and more. You will have to resist those eyes, as you could literally be killing your dog with kindness. A tasty treat of two, or three small dog biscuits at bedtime, besides their regular meals, is plenty.

Over-feeding your Cavalier leads to obesity, which, in turn, could lead to health problems. An overweight dog puts unnecessary strain on the heart and joints, and finds it difficult to get around. A vicious circle then sets in, as your dog does not want to go for walks or play games, and will become very lethargic. A healthy Cavalier is neither too thin nor too fat. When you gently run your hands over the ribcage, you should be able to feel each rib – but not be able to see them. Your Cavalier should appear bright-eyed and alert, and his coat should be gleaming.

permissible. This makes the coat one of the easiest to care for, and you will need minimal grooming equipment (see Chapter Four). With regular grooming and bathing, the coat will stay in good condition.

PUPPY CARE

Your puppy will need to get used to being handled daily and groomed from an early age. You will soon get into a daily routine, and it very quickly becomes part of everyday life. Start by placing the puppy on a non-slip surface. Ideally, position a rubber-backed mat on a secure work surface or table, and keep a firm hold so that the puppy does not fall.

Start by using a soft bristle brush, which can be purchased from your local pet store, and brush gently from the head in the direction that the hair lies. Then brush gently downwards on the ears. Your puppy will soon become accustomed to being handled in this way and will look forward to his grooming sessions.

- **Eyes:** Clean your puppy's eyes with a proprietary eye cleaner; cotton make-up removal pads are ideal for this purpose. Wet a clean pad in the solution and gently wipe the eye, using a separate pad for each eye. Then use fresh pads to dry each eye after cleaning.
- **Ears:** You will also need to get your puppy used to having his ears checked weekly. Gently lift each ear and examine the inside for dirt or debris. If necessary, the ears can be cleaned by very gently wiping around the ear opening, using a saline solution. This can be made at home using one tablespoon of salt to one pint (550 ml) of warm water.

Use a fresh cotton pad for each ear, and squeeze as much moisture from the pad as possible. Do not push the pads or prod into the ear, as this can be very dangerous and cause damage. Never use a cotton bud – if it is pushed down too far, it can perforate the ear drum.

It shouldn't be necessary to treat a puppy's ears for ear mites, but if you do find your puppy has them, it is best to seek veterinary advice rather than using something purchased over the counter at a pet store, which may be unsuitable for young puppies. As your puppy gets older, you can obtain an ear cleaning solution from your veterinary surgeon. Follow the

HANDLING A PUPPY

A puppy needs to get used to all-over handling so he is happy to be groomed and will accept an examination by a vet.

A puppy should feel completely relaxed when he is being handled.

Pick up each paw in turn.

Open the mouth to check gums and teeth.

manufacturer's instructions and, when used weekly, this should keep your dog's ears free from problems.

• **Teeth:** Your puppy's teeth will also need regular checks. Get your puppy used to this by wrapping a clean wet cotton pad around your index finger and applying a small amount of toothpaste that has been specifically designed for dogs. Gently rub around the puppy's teeth and then reward him for co-operating. After a few weeks, you can start using a soft toothbrush; a baby's toothbrush is ideal at this stage.

At approximately four to five months, your puppy will start to lose his puppy teeth and his adult teeth will break through. Your puppy's mouth and gums will become tender at this time, so gentle handling and brushing will be necessary.

• **Nails:** Check your puppy's nails. He should wear his nails down by walking on hard surfaces when out for his walks, but sometimes it may be necessary to trim the nails. There are several nail clippers on the market; choose the ones that you feel most comfortable using. When cutting the nails remember not to cut above the quick; this can cause bleeding and be quite painful. After you have trimmed the nail, gently rub over the clipped area with the nail file. This will take off any sharpness and prevent any scratches to other dogs or children if the dog jumps up.

ADULT CARE
Keep to the same regime as when your Cavalier was a puppy, checking and cleaning his eyes

ROUTINE CARE

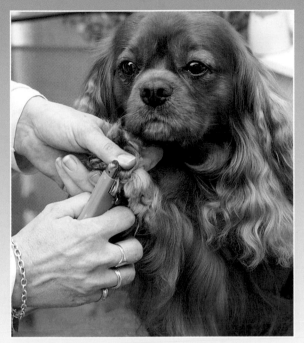

Nails will need to be trimmed on a regular basis.

The teeth should be checked, and cleaned when necessary.

and ears. When checking the nails, look underneath for matted hair between the pads. You will need to trim the hair away, using a small rounded-end scissors, taking care not to cut the pad.

Clean your Cavalier's teeth once a week, with a medium bristle toothbrush. At the same time, check the gums for redness. A build-up of plaque can lead to severe periodontal (gum) disease. This is extremely painful and can make eating very difficult, and sometimes impossible, which will affect your dog's general health.

Grooming a Cavalier is easy and

your Cavalier will enjoy the extra attention. If you groom regularly, it will only take a few minutes for a puppy and 5-10 minutes for an adult. A neglected coat will take much longer to sort out. It is then that grooming becomes a chore for you and can be very painful for your dog.

To keep your Cavalier's coat looking and feeling its best, grooming should be done on a regular daily basis – at least twice a week. Twice a year your dog will shed his coat; at this time you will need to groom your Cavalier on a daily basis to keep the coat

free from knots and tangles.

If your Cavalier is neutered, the coat may thicken, and it will take a little more effort to keep in good condition. In this instance, daily grooming is essential. Apart from the weekly groom, which is best carried out on a tabletop, it can be therapeutic for both dog and human to gently brush your Cavalier while you are sitting on the sofa, watching the television.

During the winter months, Cavaliers can come home looking very dirty and muddy from their walks. Most of the time a little dirt will soon fall out of a silky well-groomed coat, but sometimes the dirt and debris needs a little extra attention. You can clean the coat by using a no-rinse shampoo, applying it liberally, rubbing it into the coat, and towelling dry. Alternatively, you can stand your Cavalier in a sink and thoroughly wash and dry the legs and undercarriage.

GROOMING ROUTINE

When you are grooming your Cavalier, adopt the following routine to ensure you work through the entire coat:

- Start at the chest, using the slicker brush.
- Lift each front leg and brush the feathering. Make sure you brush under each front leg, as mats can form easily in this area if ignored. Brush thoroughly, gently teasing small mats out between the fingers.
- Brush the ears, paying particular attention to the area at the back of the ears nearest the head. Turn the earflap and brush the inside of the ears thoroughly.
- Work down the body towards the tail and each side of the dog.
- Brush the tail thoroughly, and then work down the back of the legs.
- Check underneath each foot. If the hair is growing too thickly between the pads, trim the hair

TOP TIP

Add a daily supplement of cod liver oil in the winter. This contains omega3 fatty acids, with vitamins A and D, which help to keep joints supple and promote strong bones. Do not give this in the summer, as it can irritate your dog's skin. In the autumn, spring and summer months, give evening primrose oil capsules or a little corn oil, which promotes a healthy skin and coat, and helps to alleviate dry skin conditions.

using round-ended scissors.
- After brushing the coat with a slicker brush, gently go through the coat with a medium-tooth comb, paying particular attention to the ears, chest feathering, undercarriage, tail and leg featherings.
- Finish by using a pure bristle brush over the coat. This helps to produce a nice shine, and the bristles will help to elevate any static in the coat.
- If your Cavalier's coat is a little flyaway, slightly dampen the brush and this should help settle the coat. Alternatively, use a grooming spray, which is perfumed and helps keep your Cavalier smelling sweet. Never spray directly on to the coat, as many sprays are oil-based. Spray sparingly on to the brush, and gently work through the body of the coat.

BATHING

Occasionally you will need to bath your Cavalier to keep his coat in good condition and to make sure he smells fresh and sweet. How often you bath your dog depends on you and your dog's lifestyle, but regular bathing, on a monthly basis, should be sufficient to keep your Cavalier's coat silky and gleaming.

Make sure you use a specially formulated shampoo and conditioner for dogs. There are many different products on the market: some are cleansing and beautifying shampoos; some are combined with conditioners; others contain flea-repellent insecticides to deter any unwanted visitors. Do not use insecticidal shampoos on puppies. There are plenty of puppy shampoos to choose from, which are gentle on a sensitive skin and do not sting if it gets into a puppy's eyes. If you need to use a flea treatment, there are a number of topical preparations that are suitable, but it is best to seek veterinary advice.

Before bathing, groom your Cavalier thoroughly, carrying out your weekly grooming regime. Make sure that the coat is free from all knots and mats; bathing a dog with a matted coat will make the tangles worse and much harder to remove.

The easiest way to bath a Cavalier is to use a shower

GROOMING PROCEDURE

Use a slicker brush to work through the coat. Pay particular attention to the feathering on the legs.

The feathering on the ears may become matted or tangled.

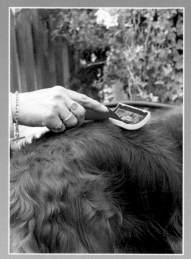

Work your way along the back, brushing with the lay of the coat.

The undercarriage will need attention.

The Cavalier has a beautiful feathered tail, which needs to be tangle-free.

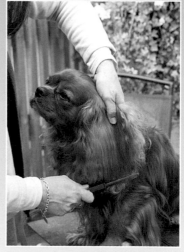

Once you have finished brushing, you will need to comb through the coat.

Regular bathing will help to keep your Cavalier's coat in top condition.

SHOW DOGS

If you show your Cavalier, keeping the coat in tip-top condition is paramount – and this means lots of hard work. The day before a show, exhibitors bath and groom their dogs in preparation for the next day. But, in truth, grooming a show dog must be done on a daily basis in order to keep the coat and featherings clean and tangle-free. Males especially need to have their legs and undercarriage washed daily to prevent urine stains from forming.

Exhibitors of whole colours will often bathe their Cavaliers midway between shows rather than the night before, as this gives time for the natural oils to return to the coat to produce a beautiful sheen. However, the undercarriage and leg featherings will be washed the night before a show.

attachment on the hot and cold tap in the bath. Your dog will be happier if he is standing on a non-slip rubber mat.

- Start by putting a cotton wool ball in each ear to stop any excess water getting into the ear canal.
- Mix the shampoo in a jug with warm water, approximately one part shampoo to 10 parts water, or to the manufacturer's recommended instructions.
- Make sure the water is at the correct temperature, and then thoroughly wet the coat.
- Tilt your Cavalier's head slightly backwards and pour the shampoo mixture on to the coat from the back of the neck down the body. Take care not to get any shampoo into the dog's eyes.
- Rub the shampoo into the coat to make a rich lather.
- Rinse the coat and then repeat.
- Squeeze the excess water from the coat, and then apply conditioner, gently working it in with your fingertips.
- Comb through the coat and rinse thoroughly, making sure you have removed all the conditioner.
- Squeeze the excess water from the dog's coat and towel dry until the coat is just damp.
- Remove the cotton wool balls if they haven't already been shaken out.
- Blow dry the coat, using a hairdryer on a warm setting and medium speed. Start with the ears and chest, and then

An adult Cavalier will enjoy as much exercise as you give him.

work through the rest of the coat, making sure your Cavalier is dry under each leg. It is important to dry your Cavalier thoroughly so he doesn't catch a chill. In the summer months, on a nice warm day, your Cavalier will enjoy drying naturally.

EXERCISE

Once your puppy has completed his vaccination programme, he will be ready to go out into the big, wide world. Cavaliers, like any other dogs, love going for walks and will enjoy accompanying their owners on family outings to the beach. Do make sure that the beach you are visiting does not have a 'no dogs' policy in the summer months (usually March to October).

Many Cavaliers love water and enjoy swimming, and will head straight for water when they are out on walks. They also like rambles through the woods, and love nothing more than to pick up the scent of woodland animals. If you live in a more urban environment, your Cavalier will be perfectly happy with a walk in the local park.

Exercise is good for the mind, body and soul, stimulating the brain and building muscle tone and making your Cavalier a healthier, happier dog. Adult Cavaliers are capable of going on long walks, but do be careful of over-walking puppies. A Cavalier under six months of age cannot tolerate long walks. Besides tiring him out, you need to bear in mind that a puppy is going through his maximum growth stage, and over-exercise can damage growing bones and growth plates.

Start your puppy with short walks – no more than 5-10 minutes – and gradually build up to more moderate exercise over a period of six months. Your puppy will also be getting free-running exercise in the garden, and so going out for walks is more important for socialisation than for exercise purposes. Once your Cavalier has reached maturity then he can participate in long walks and rambles freely, and this will be one of the great pleasures of owning a dog.

Keeping your Cavalier's mind active and stimulated adds to his wellbeing. As well as taking him for walks, teach him to retrieve. This is a fun form of exercise, and your Cavalier will enjoy

As your Cavalier grows older, you need to be aware of his changing needs.

You may find that an older Cavalier loses a little weight. Dividing the food ration into two meals per day is easier on the system. Also, at this time, he may not be able to go through the night without relieving himself. If your Cavalier has an accident, sympathise with his needs, maybe by putting down some newspaper or puppy pads, which can be purchased on the internet or at pet shops.

As your Cavalier gets older his exercise needs will decrease slightly. Some dogs are able to cope with any amount of exercise, but some older dogs slow down and their tolerance levels fall. Never force an older dog to walk for long periods if he is not capable of doing so – as with puppies, this will do more harm than good. Let him tell you how much he is capable of, and sometimes he just might like to potter.

It could be that your dog's joints have stiffened with age, and pressure on the joints may be painful. There are many products on the market that help to ease stiffness; ask your vet for advice. Hydrotherapy is an excellent form of exercise for the older dog. It is non-weight bearing, and doesn't put any unnecessary strain on the joints, but it keeps the dog exercising, maintaining good circulation, and also keeps his mind stimulated.

This is also a very good form of exercise for dogs that have undergone any form of joint surgery. Billy, one of our rescued

interacting with you. You can also buy rubber toys that can be filled with food and these keep dogs amused for hours, but remember to deduct the food you use from your dog's daily ration.

SPECIAL NEEDS
Many Cavaliers live long and active lives into their teens. At this time a little more care and consideration needs to be given.

You will need to check an older dog's teeth on a weekly basis at your regular grooming session. The teeth must be kept clean and free from tartar build-up. If your Cavalier develops an excess of tartar, which you cannot remove, seek veterinary advice, as periodontal disease is very painful. Teeth may also become loose, which could cause problems, making eating very difficult.

Cavaliers, came to us with a huge cancerous lump on his leg, which, unfortunately, had to be amputated. Once his stitches had been removed we took him for hydrotherapy sessions to build up the muscles in his remaining three legs. He enjoyed these sessions very much and used to pull very excitedly towards the pool. When let off the lead, he would run up the ramp and jump straight into the water – not waiting for his harness to be put on.

SAYING GOODBYE

In an ideal world, we would prefer the awful decision for the passing of our pets to be taken out of our hands, and for them to pass peacefully away in their sleep. Unfortunately, it is not an ideal world, and sadly the day comes when a decision has to be made, and we have no alternative but to say goodbye – be it through old age or illness. This decision is never easy and we have all been there.

Often, making the right decision is between you and your vet, but ultimately it has to be your decision. Contact the surgery and ask to speak to your vet personally. In a good practice, the vet will be extremely sympathetic and will either arrange for you to take your Cavalier to the surgery or will come home to you – either way doesn't make the situation any easier to handle, but you will know in your heart when the time has come.

Some people like to bury their

In time, you will be able to look back and remember all the happy times you spent with your beloved Cavalier.

Cavalier in a special place in the garden, maybe where he loved to spend a warm sunny afternoon lazing around, or a place where you can add a flowering memorial. Others prefer to have their Cavaliers cremated and the ashes returned to keep in the house, or to place in the garden or into a plant tub, which can be transported in the event of moving house. The decision is a personal one and whichever way

you choose to remember your Cavalier has to be right for you and your family. There are many vets who are able to offer burial or cremation services through a pet crematorium, or you can choose to do this privately (see Appendices).

In time you will come to realise that peace is a parting gift and it is the last act of love and kindness you can do for the little Cavalier you loved so much.

TRAINING AND SOCIALISATION

Chapter 6

When you decided to bring a Cavalier King Charles Spaniel into your life, you probably had dreams of how it was going to be: long walks together, cosy evenings with a Cavalier curled up on your lap, and, whenever you returned home, there would always be a special welcome waiting for you.

There is no doubt that you can achieve all this – and much more – with a Cavalier, but like anything that is worth having, you must be prepared to put in the work. A Cavalier, regardless of whether it is a puppy or an adult, does not come ready trained, understanding exactly what you want and fitting perfectly into your lifestyle. A Cavalier has to learn his place in your family and he must discover what is acceptable behaviour.

We have a great starting point in that the Cavalier has an outstanding temperament. The breed was developed especially to be a companion, and so Cavaliers are loving, affectionate and eager to please.

THE FAMILY PACK

Dogs have been domesticated for some 14,000 years, but, luckily for us, they have inherited and retained behaviour from their distant ancestor – the wolf. A Cavalier King Charles Spaniel may never have lived in the wild, but he is born with the survival skills and the mentality of a meat-eating predator who hunts in a pack. A wolf living in a pack owes its existence to mutual co-operation and an acceptance of a hierarchy, as this ensures both food and protection. A domesticated dog living in a family pack has exactly the same outlook. He wants food, companionship, and leadership –

and it is your job to provide for these needs.

YOUR ROLE

Theories about dog behaviour and methods of training go in and out of fashion, but in reality nothing has changed from the day when wolves ventured in from the wild to join the family circle. The wolf (and equally the dog) accepts a subservient place in the family pack in return for food and protection. In a dog's eyes, you are his leader, and he relies on you to make all the important decisions. This does not mean that you have to act like a dictator or a bully. You are accepted as a leader, without argument, as long as you have the right credentials.

The first part of the job is easy. You are the provider, and you are therefore respected because you supply food. In a Cavalier's eyes, you must be the ultimate hunter

Do you have what it takes to be a firm, fair and consistent leader?

because a day never goes by when you cannot find food. The second part of the leader's job description is straightforward, but for some reason we find it hard to achieve. In order for a dog to accept his place in the family pack he must respect his leader as the decision-maker. A low-ranking pack animal does not question authority; he is perfectly happy to see someone else shoulder the responsibility. Problems will only arise if you cut a poor figure as leader and the dog feels he should mount a challenge for the top-ranking role.

HOW TO BE A GOOD LEADER

There are a number of guidelines to follow to establish yourself in the role of leader in a way that your Cavalier understands and respects. If you have a puppy, you may think you don't have to take this on board for a few months, but that would be a big mistake. Start as you mean to go on, and your pup will be quick to find his place in his new family.

- **Keep it simple:** Decide on the rules you want your Cavalier to obey and always make it 100 per cent clear what is acceptable, and what is unacceptable, behaviour.
- **Be consistent:** If you are not consistent about enforcing rules, how can you expect your Cavalier to take you

seriously? There is nothing worse than allowing your Cavalier to jump up at you one moment and then scolding him the next time he does it because you are wearing your best clothes. As far as the Cavalier is concerned, he may as well try it on because he can't predict your reaction.

- **Get your timing right:** If you are rewarding your Cavalier, and equally if you are reprimanding him, you must respond within one to two seconds otherwise the dog will not link his behaviour with your reaction (see page 87).
- **Read your dog's body language:** Find out how to

read body language and facial expressions (see page 86) so that you understand your Cavalier's feelings and his intentions.

- **Be aware of your own body language:** You can help your dog to learn by using your body language to communicate with him. For example, if you want your dog to come to you, open your arms out and look inviting. If you want your dog to stay, use a hand signal (palm flat, facing the dog) so you are effectively 'blocking' his advance.

- **Tone of voice:** Dogs are very receptive to tone of voice, so you can use your voice to praise him or to correct undesirable behaviour. If you are pleased with your Cavalier, praise him to the skies in a warm, happy voice. If you want to stop him raiding the bin, use a deep, stern voice when you say "No".

- **Give one command only:** If you keep repeating a command, or keeping changing it, your Cavalier will think you are babbling and will probably ignore you. If your Cavalier does not respond the first time you ask, make it simple by using a treat to lure him into position, and then you can reward him for a correct response.

- **Daily reminders:** A young Cavalier may forget his manners from time to time, but rather than coming down on your Cavalier like a ton of bricks when he does

The Cavalier is an adaptable dog and if he knows what is allowed, he will rarely seek to challenge the house rules.

something wrong, try to prevent bad manners by daily reminders of good manners. For example:

i Stick to the house rules so that your Cavalier knows what is, and what is not, allowed. If you don't want him to lie on the sofa, don't allow him to climb up for an occasional cuddle.

ii Do not let him leap out of the car the moment you open the door (which could be potentially lethal, as well as being disrespectful).

iii Do not let him eat from your hand when you are at the table.

READING BODY LANGUAGE

If you observe dogs interacting, you will begin to understand canine body language.

UNDERSTANDING YOUR CAVALIER

Body language is an important means of communication between dogs, which they use to make friends, to assert status, and to avoid conflict. It is important to get on your dog's wavelength by understanding his body language and reading his facial expressions.

• A positive body posture and a wagging tail indicate a happy, confident dog. The ever-wagging tail is a particular hallmark of the Cavalier.

• A crouched body posture with ears back and tail down show that a dog is being submissive. A dog may do this when he is being told off or if a more assertive dog approaches him.

• A bold dog will stand tall, trying to make himself look important. His ears will be forward and his tail will be held high.

• A dog who raises his hackles (lifting the fur along his topline) is trying to look as scary as possible. This can be the prelude to aggressive behaviour, but, in many cases, the dog is apprehensive and is unsure how to cope with a situation.

• A playful dog will go down on his front legs while standing on his hind legs in a bow position. This friendly invitation says: "I'm no threat, let's play."

• A nervous dog will often show aggressive behaviour as a means of self-protection. If threatened, this dog will lower his head and flatten his ears. The corners of his mouth may be drawn back, and he may bark or whine.

GIVING REWARDS

Why should your Cavalier do as you ask? If you follow the guidelines given above, your Cavalier should respect your authority, but what about the time when he is playing with a new doggy friend or has found a really enticing scent? The answer is that you must always be the most interesting, the most attractive, and the most irresistible person in your Cavalier's eyes. It would be nice to think you could achieve this by personality alone, but most of us need a little extra help. You need to find out what is the biggest reward for your dog – in a Cavalier's case it will nearly always be food. Cavaliers love their food, and they particularly relish a special treat, such as cooked chicken, cheese or liver cake. For some Cavaliers the reward might be a play with a favourite toy – squeaky toys are popular with Cavs – but, whatever it is, it must be something that your dog really wants.

When you are teaching a dog a new exercise, you should reward him frequently. When he knows the exercise or command, reward him randomly so that he keeps on responding to you in a positive manner. If your dog does something extra special, like leaving his canine chum mid-play in the park, make sure he really knows how pleased you are by giving him a handful of treats or throwing his ball a few extra

If you find a treat your Cavalier values, you will have his undivided attention.

times. If he gets a bonanza reward, he is more likely to come back on future occasions, because you have proved to be even more rewarding than his previous activity.

TOP TREATS

Some trainers grade treats depending on what they are asking the dog to do. A dog may get a low-grade treat, such as a piece of dry food, to reward good behaviour on a random basis, such as sitting when you open a door or allowing you to examine his teeth. But high-grade treats, such as chicken or cheese, are reserved for training new exercises or for use in the park when you want a really good recall. Whatever type of treat you use, remember to subtract it from your Cavalier's daily ration. Fat Cavs are lethargic, prone to health problems, and will almost certainly have a shorter life-

expectancy. Reward your Cavalier, but always keep a check on his figure!

HOW DO DOGS LEARN?

It is not difficult to get inside your Cavalier's head and understand how he learns, as it is not dissimilar to the way we learn. Dogs learn by conditioning: they find out that specific behaviours produce specific consequences. This is known as operant conditioning or consequence learning. Consequences have to be immediate or clearly linked to the behaviour, as a dog sees the world in terms of action and result. Dogs will quickly learn if an action has a bad consequence or a good consequence.

Dogs also learn by association. This is known as classical conditioning or association learning. It is the type of learning made famous by Pavlov's experiment with dogs. Pavlov presented dogs with food and measured their salivary response (how much they drooled). Then he rang a bell just before presenting the food. At first, the dogs did not salivate until the food was presented. But after a while they learnt that the sound of the bell meant that food was coming, and so they salivated when they heard the bell. A dog needs to learn the association in order for it to have any meaning. For example, a dog that has never

THE CLICKER REVOLUTION

Karen Pryor pioneered the technique of clicker training when she was working with dolphins. Karen wanted to mark 'correct' behaviour at the precise moment it happened. She found it was impossible to toss a fish to a dolphin when it was in mid-air, when she wanted to reward it. Her aim was to establish a conditioned response so the dolphin knew that it had performed correctly and a reward would follow.

The solution was the clicker: a small matchbox-shaped training aid, with a metal tongue that makes a click when it is pressed. To begin with, the dolphin had to learn that a click meant that food was coming. The dolphin then learnt that it must 'earn' a click in order to get a reward. Clicker training has been

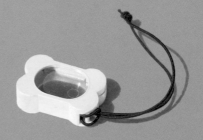

used with many different animals, most particularly with dogs, and it has proved hugely successful. It is a great aid for pet owners and is also widely used by professional trainers who teach highly specialised skills.

seen a lead before will be completely indifferent to it. A dog that has learnt that a lead means he is going for a walk will get excited the second he sees the lead; he has learnt to associate a lead with a walk.

BE POSITIVE
The most effective method of training dogs is to use their ability to learn by consequence and to teach that the behaviour you want produces a good consequence. For example, if you ask your Cavalier to "Sit", and reward him with a treat, he will learn that it is worth his while to sit on command because it will

lead to a treat. He is far more likely to repeat the behaviour, and the behaviour will become stronger, because it results in a positive outcome. This method of training is known as positive reinforcement, and it generally leads to a happy, co-operative dog that is willing to work, and a handler who has fun training their dog.

The opposite approach is negative reinforcement. This is far less effective and often results in a poor relationship between dog and owner. In this method of training, you ask your Cavalier to "Sit", and, if he does not respond, you deliver a sharp yank

on the training collar or push his rear to the ground. The dog learns that not responding to your command has a bad consequence, and he may be less likely to ignore you in the future. However, it may well have a bad consequence for you, too. A dog that is treated in this way may associate harsh handling with the handler and become fearful. Instead of establishing a pattern of willing co-operation, you are establishing a relationship built on coercion.

GETTING STARTED
As you train your Cavalier, you will develop your own techniques

as you get to know what motivates him. You may decide to get involved with clicker training or you may prefer to go for a simple command-and-reward formula. It does not matter what form of training you use, as long as it is based on positive, reward-based methods.

Cavaliers have average intelligence – although you do get some individuals that are very bright. But, in most cases, a Cavalier needs a lot of repetition in order to fully learn an exercise. He may appear to 'get it' after a few repeats, but the next time you try, he will probably have forgotten what you wanted. Calculate 30 repeats, and then you can be 100 per cent confident that your Cavalier understands the exercise.

There are a few important guidelines to bear in mind when you are training your Cavalier:

A puppy has a short attention span, so keep training sessions short – and full of fun.

- Find a training area that is free from distractions, particularly when you are just starting out.
- Keep training sessions short, especially with young puppies that have very short attention spans.
- Do not train if you are in a bad mood or if you are on a tight schedule – the training session will be doomed to failure.
- If you are using a toy as a reward, make sure it is only available when you are training. In this way it has an added value for your Cavalier.
- If you are using food treats, make sure they are bite-size and easy to swallow; you don't

want to hang about while your Cavalier chews on his treat.
- All food treats must be deducted from your Cavalier's daily food ration.
- When you are training, move around your allocated area so that your dog does not think that an exercise can only be performed in one place.
- If your Cavalier is finding an exercise difficult, try not to get frustrated. Go back a step and praise him for his effort. Repetition is key, so keep on trying in successive training sessions, and your Cavalier will be successful.
- Keep training sessions cheerful and upbeat. A Cavalier will

become depressed and morose if you become domineering in your approach. But if he thinks training is one big game, he will be happy to work for you.
- Always end training sessions on a happy, positive note. Ask your Cavalier to do something you know he can do – it could be a trick he enjoys performing – and then reward him with a few treats or an extra-long play session.

In the exercises that follow, clicker training is introduced and followed, but all the exercises will work without the use of a clicker.

INTRODUCING A CLICKER

This is dead easy, and your ever-hungry Cavalier will learn about the clicker in record time! It can be combined with attention training, which is a very useful tool and can be used on many different occasions.

- Prepare some treats and go to an area that is free from distractions. When your Cavalier stops sniffing around and looks at you, click and reward by throwing him a treat. This means he will not crowd you, but will go looking for the treat. Repeat a couple of times. If your Cavalier is very easily distracted, you may need to start this exercise with the dog on a lead.
- After a few clicks, your Cavalier understands that if he hears a click, he will get a treat. He must now learn that he must 'earn' a click. This time, when your Cavalier looks at you, wait a little longer before clicking, and then reward him. If your Cavalier is on a lead but responding well, try him off the lead.
- When your Cavalier is working for a click and giving you his attention, you can introduce a cue or command word, such as "Watch". Repeat a few times, using the cue. You now have a Cavalier that understands the clicker and will give you his attention when you ask him to "Watch".

TRAINING EXERCISES

A Cavalier will master all the following exercises over a period of time. Do not be impatient – with a Cavalier, remember that little and often will win the day.

THE SIT

This is the easiest exercise to teach, so it is rewarding for both you and your Cavalier.

- Choose a tasty treat and hold it just above your puppy's nose. As he looks up at the treat, he will naturally go into the Sit. As soon as he is in position, reward him.
- Repeat the exercise, and when your pup understands what you want, introduce the "Sit" command.
- You can practise at mealtimes by holding out the bowl and waiting for your dog to sit. Most Cavaliers learn this one very quickly!

Use a treat to lure your Cavalier into the Sit position.

THE DOWN

Work hard at this exercise because a reliable Down is useful in many different situations, and an instant Down can be a lifesaver.

Lower the treat towards the ground and your Cavalier should follow it, going into the Down position.

- You can start with your dog in a Sit, or it is just as effective to teach it when the dog is standing. Hold a treat just below your puppy's nose, and slowly lower it towards the ground. The treat acts as a lure, and your puppy will follow it, first going down on his forequarters and then bringing his hindquarters down as he tries to get the treat.
- Make sure you close your fist around the treat, and only reward your puppy with the treat when he is in the correct position. If your puppy is reluctant to go Down, you can apply gentle pressure on his shoulders to encourage him to go into the correct position.
- When your puppy is following the treat and going in to position, introduce a verbal command.
- Build up this exercise over a period of time, each time waiting a little longer before giving the reward, so the puppy learns to stay in the Down position.

THE RECALL

It is never too soon to start training the Recall. In fact, if you have a puppy, it is best to start almost from the moment he arrives home, as he has a strong instinct to follow you. Make sure you are always happy and excited when your Cavalier comes to you, even if he has been slower than you would like. Your Cavalier must believe that the greatest reward is coming to you.

- You can start teaching the Recall from the moment your puppy arrives home. He will naturally follow you, so keep calling his name and rewarding him when he comes to you.
- Practise in the garden. When your puppy is busy exploring, get his attention by calling his name. As he runs towards you, introduce the verbal command "Come". Make sure you sound happy and exciting, so your puppy wants to come to you. When he responds, give him lots of praise.
- If your puppy is slow to respond, try running away a few paces or jumping up and down. It doesn't matter how silly you look, the key issue is to get your puppy's attention – and then make yourself irresistible!
- In a dog's mind, coming when called should be regarded as the best fun because he knows he is always going to be rewarded. Never make the mistake of telling your dog off, no matter how slow he is to respond, as you will undo all your previous hard work.
- When you are free-running your dog, make sure you have his favourite toy or a pocket full of treats so you can reward him at intervals throughout the walk when you call him to you. Do not allow your dog to run free and only call him back at the end of the walk to clip on his lead. A Cavalier will

CALLING YOUR CAVALIER

Make sure you have your Cavalier's attention and then call him to you.

Try to make yourself sound exciting so your Cavalier wants to come to you.

soon realise that the Recall means the end of his walk, and then end of fun – so who can blame him for not wanting to come back?

TRAINING LINE

This is the equivalent of a very long lead, which you can buy at a pet store, or you can make your own with a length of rope. The training line is attached to your Cavalier's collar and should be around 15 feet (4.5 metres) in length.

The purpose of the training line is to prevent your Cavalier from disobeying you so that he never has the chance to get into bad habits. For example, when you call your Cavalier and he ignores you, you can immediately pick

up the end of the training line and call him again. By picking up the line you will have attracted his attention, and if you call in an excited, happy voice, your Cavalier will come to you. The moment he comes to you, give him a tasty treat so he is instantly rewarded for making the 'right' decision. You may find that it helps to use a squeaky toy to attract your Cavalier's attention, and this will give him additional incentive to come to you.

The training line is very useful when your Cavalier becomes an adolescent and is testing your leadership. When you have reinforced the correct behaviour a number of times, your dog will build up a strong recall and you will not need to use the line.

WALKING ON A LOOSE LEAD

This is a simple exercise, and it should be straightforward with a relatively small dog. However, many Cavalier owners get into difficulties because they are too impatient, wanting to get on with the expedition rather that training the dog how to walk on a lead. Take time with this one; a Cavalier that walks nicely on a loose lead is a pleasure to take out, and you are therefore more likely to take him on expeditions, which will make his life more interesting.

• In the early stages of lead training, allow your puppy to pick his route and follow him. He will get used to the feeling of being 'attached' to you, and will have no reason to resist.

SECRET WEAPON

You can build up a strong Recall by using another form of association learning. Buy a whistle and peep on it when you are giving your Cavalier his food. You can choose the type of signal you want to give: two short peeps or one long whistle, for example. Within a matter of days, your dog will learn that the sound of the whistle means that food is coming.

Now transfer the lesson outside. Arm yourself with some tasty treats and the whistle. Allow your Cavalier to run free in the garden, and, after a couple of minutes, use the whistle. The dog has already learnt to associate the whistle with food, so he will come towards you. Immediately reward him with a treat and lots of praise. Repeat the lesson a few times in the garden so you are confident that your dog is responding before trying it in the park. Make sure you always have some treats in your pocket when you go for a walk, and your dog will quickly learn how rewarding it is to come to you.

- Next, show your puppy that you have a tasty treat, and then let him follow the treat for a few paces before rewarding him.
- Build up the amount of time your pup will walk with you, and, when he is walking nicely by your side, introduce the verbal command "Heel" or "Close". Give lots of praise when your pup is in the correct position.
- When your pup is walking alongside you, keep focusing his attention on you by using his name, and then reward him when he looks at you. If it is going well, introduce some changes of direction.
- Do not attempt to take your puppy out on the lead until

The aim is for your Cavalier to walk beside you on a loose lead.

you have mastered the basics at home. You need to be confident that your puppy accepts the lead and will focus his attention on you, when requested, before you face the challenge of a busy environment.

- Your Cavalier may try to pull on the lead, particularly if you are heading somewhere he wants to go, such as the park. If this happens, stop, call your dog to you, and do not set off again until he is in the correct position. It may take time, but your Cavalier will eventually realise that it is more productive to walk by your side than to pull ahead.

STAYS

This may not be the most exciting exercise, but it is one of the most useful. There are many occasions when you want your Cavalier to stay in position, even if it is only for a few seconds. The classic example is when you want your Cavalier to stay in the back of the car until you have clipped on his lead. Some trainers use the verbal command "Stay" when the dog is to stay in position for an extended period of time, and "Wait" if the dog is to stay in position for a few seconds until you give the next

A well-trained Cavalier is a pleasure to own.

command. Others trainers use a universal "Stay" to cover all situations. It all comes down to personal preference; as long as you are consistent, your dog will understand the command he is given.

- Put your puppy in a Sit or a Down, and use a handsignal (flat palm, facing the dog) to show he is to stay in position. Step a pace away from the dog. Wait a second, step back and reward him. If you have a lively pup, you may find it easier to train this exercise on the lead.
- Repeat the exercise, gradually increasing the distance you can

leave your dog. When you return to your dog's side, praise him quietly, and release him with a command, such as "OK".

- Remember to keep your body language very still when you are training this exercise, and avoid eye contact with your dog. Work on this exercise over a period of time, and you will build up a really reliable Stay.

SOCIALISATION

While your Cavalier is mastering basic obedience exercises, there is other, equally important, work to do with him. A Cavalier is not only becoming a part of your home and family, he is becoming a member of the community. He needs to be able to live in the outside world, coping calmly with every new situation that comes his way. It is your job to introduce him to as many different experiences as possible, and encourage him to behave in an appropriate manner.

In order to socialise your Cavalier effectively, it is helpful to understand how his brain is developing, and then you will get a perspective on how he sees the world.

CANINE SOCIALISATION
(Birth to 7 weeks)
This is the time when a dog learns

These Cavalier puppies are receiving the benefit of additional socialisation from a kindly German Shepherd.

how to be a dog. By interacting with his mother and his littermates, a young pup learns about leadership and submission. He learns to read body posture so that he understands the intentions of his mother and his siblings. A puppy that is taken away from his litter too early may always have behavioural problems with other dogs, either being fearful or aggressive.

SOCIALISATION PERIOD
(7 to 12 weeks)

This is the time to get cracking and introduce your Cavalier puppy to as many different experiences as possible. This includes meeting different people, other dogs and animals, seeing new sights, and hearing a range of sounds, from the vacuum cleaner to the roar of

traffic. At this stage, a puppy learns very quickly and what he learns will stay with him for the rest of his life. This is the best time for a puppy to move to a new home, as he is adaptable and ready to form deep bonds.

FEAR-IMPRINT PERIOD
(8 to 11 weeks)

This occurs during the socialisation period, and it can be the cause of problems if it is not handled carefully. If a pup is exposed to a frightening or painful experience, it will lead to lasting impressions. Obviously, you will attempt to avoid frightening situations, such as your pup being bullied by a mean-spirited older dog or a firework going off, but you cannot always protect your puppy from the unexpected. If

your pup has a nasty experience, the best plan is to make light of it and distract him by offering him a treat or a game. The pup will take the lead from you and will be reassured that there is nothing to worry about. If you mollycoddle him and sympathise with him, he is far more likely to retain the memory of his fear.

SENIORITY PERIOD
(12 to 16 weeks)

During this period, your Cavalier puppy starts to cut the apron strings and becomes more independent. He will test out his status to find out who is the pack leader: him or you. Bad habits, such as play biting, which may have been seen as endearing a few weeks earlier, should be firmly discouraged. Remember to use positive, reward-based training, but make sure your puppy knows that you are the leader and must be respected.

SECOND FEAR-IMPRINT PERIOD (6 to 14 months)

This period is not as critical as the first fear-imprint period, but it should still be handled carefully. During this time your Cavalier may appear apprehensive, or he may show fear of something familiar. You may feel as if you have taken a backwards step, but if you adopt a calm, positive manner, your Cavalier will see that there is nothing to be frightened of. Do not make your dog confront the thing that frightens him. Simply distract his attention, and give him something else to think about, such as obeying a simple command, such as "Sit" or "Down". This will give you the opportunity to praise and reward your dog, and will help to boost his confidence.

YOUNG ADULTHOOD AND MATURITY (1 to 4 years)

The timing of this phase depends on the size of the dog: the bigger the dog, the later it is. This period coincides with a dog's increased size and strength, mental as well as physical. Some dogs, particularly those with a dominant nature, will test your leadership again and may become aggressive towards other dogs. Firmness and continued training are essential at this time so that your Cavalier accepts his status in the family pack.

IDEAS FOR SOCIALISATION

When you are socialising your Cavalier you want him to experience as many different situations as possible. Some Cavaliers may be a little shy to begin with. This is not a sign of poor temperament, but some dogs need more time to socialise and to gain confidence.

If you are taking on a rescued dog and have little knowledge of his background, it is important to work through a programme of socialisation. A young puppy soaks up new experiences like a sponge, but an older dog can still learn. If a rescued dog shows fear or apprehension, treat him in exactly the same way as you would treat a youngster who is going through the second fear-imprint period (see above).

Try out some of the following ideas, which will ensure your Cavalier has an all-round education.

A Cavalier that is exposed to a variety of different situations will be calm and confident.

A well-socialised Cavalier will take every new situation in his stride.

- Accustom your puppy to household noises, such as the vacuum cleaner, the television and the washing machine.
- Ask visitors to come to the door, wearing different types of clothing – for example, wearing a hat or a long raincoat, or carrying a stick or an umbrella.
- If you do not have children at home, make sure your Cavalier has a chance to meet and play with them. Go to a local park and watch children in the play area. You will not be able to take your Cavalier inside the play area, but he will see children playing and will get used to their shouts of excitement.
- Attend puppy classes. These are designed for puppies between the ages of 12 to 20 weeks, and give puppies a chance to play and interact

together in a controlled, supervised environment. Your vet will have details of a local class.
- Take a walk around some quiet streets, such as a residential area, so your Cavalier can get used to the sound of traffic. As he becomes more confident, progress to busier areas.
- Go to a railway station. You don't have to get on a train if you don't need to, but your Cavalier will have the chance to experience trains, people wheeling luggage, loudspeaker announcements, and going up and down stairs and over railway bridges.
- If you live in the town, plan a trip to the country. You can enjoy a day out and your Cavalier will get to see livestock, such as sheep, cattle and horses.

- One of the best places for socialising a dog is at a country fair. There will be crowds of people, livestock in pens, tractors, bouncy castles, fairground rides and food stalls.
- When your dog is over 20 weeks of age, find a training class for adult dogs. You may find that your local training class has both puppy and adult classes.

TRAINING CLUBS
There are lots of training clubs to choose from. Your vet will probably have details of clubs in your area, or you can ask friends who have dogs if they attend a club. Alternatively, use the internet to find out more information. But how do you know if the club is any good?

Before you take your dog, ask

if you can go to a class as an observer and find out the following:

- What experience does the instructor(s) have?
- Do they have experience with Cavaliers?
- Is the class well organised, and are the dogs reasonably quiet? (A noisy class indicates an unruly atmosphere, which will not be conducive to learning.)
- Are there are a number of

classes to suit dogs of different ages and abilities?
- Are positive, reward-based training methods used?
- Does the club train for the Good Citizen Scheme (see page 103).

If you are not happy with the training club, find another one. An inexperienced instructor who cannot handle a number of dogs in a confined environment can do more harm than good.

The adolescent Cavalier may temporarily 'forget' his good manners.

THE ADOLESCENT CAVALIER

Adolescence is the transitional period when a Cavalier is no longer a puppy, but he has yet to reach full maturity. It is hard to generalise about the onset of adolescence, as it seems to vary widely depending on breeding lines – and even between individuals in the same litter. A Cavalier male may reach adolescence at seven or eight months, but he may be as late as 11 months. A female Cavalier will generally have her first season at seven or eight months, but it may be as early as six months, or as late as 14 months.

In most cases, a male Cavalier will not change dramatically in personality at this time. Cavaliers are always affectionate, but an adolescent male may be a little more clingy. Female Cavaliers often become obsessed with toys during a season, and a bitch may select a favourite toy and carry it everywhere with her, even taking it to bed.

Just like a teenager, an adolescent Cavalier may behave erratically – sometimes breaking rules for no good reason or becoming more fearful and apprehensive. Your response must be firm, fair and consistent. Adopt a no-nonsense approach so your Cavalier does not try to play you up, and make sure you always reward good behaviour so that your Cavalier is getting positive messages from you.

WHEN THINGS GO WRONG
Positive, reward-based training

has proved to be the most effective method of teaching dogs, but what happens when your Cavalier does something wrong and you need to show him that his behaviour is unacceptable? The old-fashioned school of dog training used to rely on the powers of punishment and negative reinforcement. A dog who raided the bin, for example, was smacked. Now we have learnt that it is not only unpleasant and cruel to hit a dog, it is also ineffective. If you hit a dog for stealing, he is more than likely to see you as the bad consequence of stealing, so he may raid the bin again, but probably not when you are around. If he raided the bin some time before you discovered it, he will be even more confused by your punishment, as he will not relate your response to his 'crime'.

A more commonplace example is when a dog fails to respond to a recall in the park. When the dog eventually comes back, the owner puts the dogs on the lead and goes straight home to punish the dog for his poor response. Unfortunately, the dog will have a different interpretation. He does not think: "I won't ignore a recall command because the bad consequence is the end of my play in the park." He thinks: "Coming to my owner resulted in the end of playtime – therefore coming to my owner has a bad consequence, so I won't do that again."

There are a number of strategies to tackle undesirable behaviour – and they have nothing to do with harsh handling.

Ignoring bad behaviour: This is probably the most effective training strategy with a Cavalier. A Cavalier adores people, and the worst scenario for him is to be ignored. For example, a young Cavalier that repeatedly jumps up at visitors soon becomes a nuisance. The Cavalier is seeking attention, and so the best plan is to ignore him. Do not look at him, do not speak to him, and do not push him down – all these actions are rewarding for a Cavalier. But someone who turns their back on him and offers no response is plain boring. The moment your Cavalier has four feet on the ground, give him lots of praise and maybe a treat. If you repeat this often enough, the Cavalier will learn that jumping up does not have any good consequences, such as getting attention. Instead he is ignored. However, when he has all four feet on the ground, he gets loads of attention. He links the action with the consequence, and chooses the action that is most rewarding.

You will find that this strategy works well with all attention-seeking behaviour, such as barking, whining or scrabbling at doors. You do not need to punish a Cavalier; withdrawing your attention from him is the worst punishment he can receive. This

Ignoring attention-seeking behaviour, such as jumping up, is an effective training tool.

does not mean that you give up caring for your Cavalier, but you do not give him the extra-special attention that he craves.

Stopping bad behaviour: There are occasions when you want to

Do not allow your Cavalier to become picky about his food.

call an instant halt to whatever it is your Cavalier is doing – for example, if you have caught him red-handed in the rubbish bin. He has already committed the 'crime', so your aim is to stop him and to redirect his attention. You can do this by using a deep, firm tone of voice to say "No", which will startle him, and then call him to you in a bright, happy voice. If necessary, you can attract him with a toy or a treat. The moment your Cavalier stops the undesirable behaviour and comes towards you, you can reward his good behaviour. You can back this up by running through a couple of simple exercises, such as a Sit or a Down, and rewarding with treats. In this way, your Cavalier focuses his attention on you, and sees you as the greatest source of reward and pleasure.

PROBLEM BEHAVIOUR

If you have trained your Cavalier from puppyhood, survived his adolescence and established yourself as a fair and consistent leader, you will end up with a brilliant companion dog. The Cavalier is an easy-going, well-balanced dog who wants nothing more than to be with his people.

However, problems may arise unexpectedly, or you may have taken on a rescued Cavalier that has established behavioural problems. If you are worried about your Cavalier and feel out of your depth, do not delay in seeking professional help. This is readily available, usually through a referral from your vet, or you can find additional information on the internet (see Appendices for web addresses). An animal behaviourist will have experience

in tackling problem behaviour and will be able to help both you and your dog.

In fact, the most common cause of behavioural problems among Cavaliers is their owners! Unfortunately, many people see the charming little Cavalier more as a child than a dog – it is a mistake shared by many owners of Toy dogs. You can love your Cavalier to bits, but it is essential to remember that he is a dog, and a dog needs discipline, training and exercise as well as love and affection. If a Cavalier is never disciplined, he becomes like a pushy child and will get his own way in everything he tries.

FADDY FEEDERS

Cavalier loves their food, but a spoilt dog may become a faddy feeder if he thinks he can play you up until he is only fed the tastiest morsels of cooked chicken. Before long, you are running yourself ragged, trying to find something new for your dog to savour. Remember that you are in control, and a Cavalier needs you to make decisions for his own wellbeing.

If you believe you may have a faddy eater, check that your dog is not unwell, that his stools are normal, and that he doesn't have a sensitivity to what you are feeding him. For example, if you change food, or introduce something your dog has not had before, he may well become less enthusiastic about his food, or it may not agree with him. So, with any food change, make the switch gradually by introducing a little of the new food at a time.

If you are feeding a puppy the diet he has been given by his breeder, and he is reluctant to eat, check the following:

• Does he have a suitable bowl? A small puppy may struggle to eat from a deep bowl.

• Is the food well mixed up and sufficiently moist?

• Are you feeding too much for your puppy's requirements?

• Is your puppy teething? This occurs at any time between 14-22 weeks, and a pup's mouth may be quite sore at this time.

If you are confident that there is no reason for your puppy refusing to eat, put his food bowl down when a meal is due, and leave him alone with it for approximately 15 minutes. If he has not touched it, try feeding him a little by hand. If he still refuses to eat, pick up the bowl and take it away. Do not be tempted to give him a tasty morsel, as the chances are he will eat the treat and then refuse his next meal to see what other goodies you might have for him.

At the next feeding time, present the bowl again. Leave it for 15 minutes – then remove. This practice might go on for one or two days, but, if you persevere, you will win. If food has been refused, you can re-offer it once

A Cavalier that is not used to being left alone may become anxious.

(in the space of half a day), but then it should be thrown away. Keep the uneaten food in the fridge until the next meal is due.

If you are feeding an all-in-one complete diet, try adding a heaped teaspoon of grated cheddar cheese. If you mix this in with the complete food, it will help to get the taste buds going! Other options include adding half a boiled egg, a dessertspoon of tinned dog food, or a little chopped chicken that has been cooked. A 'topping' such as this will encourage your dog to eat, but you are not falling into the

trap of offering him new delicacies to tempt his appetite. Do not get stressed by a dog that is not eating – keep the mood lighthearted – and make sure treats are only offered after mealtimes. You can also try changing the time you feed, and introduce a slightly different routine.

Remember, a dog will not starve himself – but if you have no positive response after two days, you may want to seek veterinary advice.

SEPARATION ANXIETY
The Cavalier is a people dog, and should never be left alone for lengthy periods. He will tolerate three to four hours on his own, as long as this is not on a daily basis. A Cavalier that is left on his own for too long will become depressed and increasingly sedentary and joyless. Some Cavaliers may become destructive, and there are some that will lick at their feet until they become sore.

It is important to accustom your Cavalier to short periods of separation so that he does not become anxious. A new puppy should be left for short periods on his own, ideally in a crate where he cannot get up to any mischief. It is a good idea to leave him with a boredom-busting toy (such as a kong) so he will be happily occupied in your absence. When you return, do not rush to the crate and make a huge fuss. Wait a few minutes, and then calmly go to the crate and release your dog, telling him how good he has been. If this scenario is repeated a number of times, your Cavalier will soon learn that being left on his own is no big deal.

If your Cavalier shows signs of separation anxiety, there are a number of steps you can take:

- Put up a baby-gate between adjoining rooms, and leave your dog in one room while you are in the other room. Your dog will be able to see you and hear you, but he is learning to cope without being right next to you. Build up the amount of time you can leave your dog in easy stages.
- Buy some boredom-busting toys and fill them with some tasty treats. Whenever you leave your dog, give him a food-filled toy so that he is busy while you are away.
- If you have not used a crate before, it is not too late to start. Make sure the crate is big and comfortable, and train your Cavalier to get used to going in his crate while you are in the same room. Gradually build up the amount of time he spends in the crate, and then start leaving the room for short periods. When you return, do

Sometimes a Cavalier may become attached to a toy and resent giving it up.

not make a fuss of your dog. Leave him for five or 10 minutes before releasing him so that he gets used to your comings and goings.

- Pretend to go out, putting on your coat and jangling your keys, but do not leave the house. An anxious dog often becomes hyped up by the ritual of leave taking, and so this will help to desensitize him.
- When you go out, leave a radio or a TV on. Some dogs are comforted by hearing voices and background noise when they are left alone.
- Try to make your absences as short as possible when you are first training your dog to accept being on his own. When you return, do not rush to his crate

to release him. Leave him for a few minutes, and greet him calmly.

If you take these steps, your dog should become less anxious, and, over a period of time, you should be able to solve the problem. However, if you are failing to make progress, do not delay in calling in expert help.

POSSESSIVENESS
The Cavalier does not have a dominant nature and is rarely challenging in his behaviour. However, he does have a possessive streak, and this is generally with regard to toys. In most cases, a Cavalier will adopt a toy for a few weeks, and will then give up on it and look for something new. Many Cavalier households have a toy box, and the dogs are free to help themselves.

A problem may arise if a Cavalier becomes too attached to a toy and resents any interference with it. This is unlikely to happen if you have trained your Cavalier to give up his toys on request. But if you see signs of possessiveness, try the following:

- Restrict access to the toy box, and only allow your Cavalier to have toys when you are there to supervise.

- Teach him to 'trade' his toy, either for another toy or for a treat.
- Teach him to retrieve his toy, waiting for you to throw it, and then bringing it back and presenting it to you. This gives a structure to playing with toys, and you remain in charge.

NEW CHALLENGES

If you enjoy training your Cavalier, you may want to try one of the many dog sports that are now on offer.

Showing is highly competitive, but can be very rewarding if you have a top-quality Cavalier.

GOOD CITIZEN SCHEME

This is a scheme run by the Kennel Club in the UK and the American Kennel Club in the USA. The schemes promote responsible ownership and help you to train a well-behaved dog who will fit in with the community. The schemes are excellent for all pet owners, and they are also a good starting point if you plan to compete with your Cavalier when he is older. The KC and the AKC schemes vary in format. In the UK there are three levels: bronze, silver and gold, with each test becoming progressively more demanding. In the AKC scheme there is a single test.

Some of the exercises include:
- Walking on a loose lead among people and other dogs.
- Recall amid distractions.
- A controlled greeting where dogs stay under control while owners meet.

- The dog allows all-over grooming and handling by his owner, and also accepts being handled by the examiner.
- Stays, with the owner in sight and then out of sight.
- Food manners, allowing the owner to eat without begging, and taking a treat on command.
- Sendaway – sending the dog to his bed.

The tests are designed to show the control you have over your dog, and his ability to respond correctly and remain calm in all situations. The Good Citizen Scheme is taught at most training clubs. For more information, log on to the Kennel Club or AKC website (see Appendices).

SHOWING

In your eyes, your Cavalier is the most beautiful dog in the world – but would a judge agree? Showing is a highly competitive

sport and as the Cavalier is so popular, classes tend to be very big. However, many owners get bitten by the showing bug, and their calendar is governed by the dates of the top showing fixtures.

To be successful in the show ring, a Cavalier must conform as closely as possible to the Breed Standard, which is a written blueprint describing the 'perfect' Cavalier (see Chapter Seven). To get started, you need to buy a puppy that has show potential and then train him to perform in the ring.

A Cavalier will be expected to stand in show pose, gait for the judge in order to show off his natural movement, and to be examined by the judge. This involves a detailed hands-on examination, so your Cavalier must be bombproof when handled by strangers.

Many training clubs hold ringcraft classes, which are run by experienced showgoers. At these

AGILITY STAR
The Cavalier may be a Toy dog, but he stands up to the rigours of agility.

Powering through the tunnel.

Negotiating the weaves.

classes, you will learn how to handle your Cavalier in the ring, and you will also find out about rules, procedures and show ring etiquette.

The best plan is to start off at some small, informal shows where you can practise and learn the tricks of the trade before graduating to bigger shows. It's a long haul starting in the very first puppy class, but the dream is to make your Cavalier up into a Champion.

COMPETITIVE OBEDIENCE
Border Collies and German Shepherds dominate this sport, but there is no reason why you should not have a go with your Cavalier and see how far you can get. The classes start off being relatively easy and become progressively more challenging, with additional exercises and the handler giving minimal instructions to the dog.

Exercises include:

- **Heelwork:** Dog and handler must complete a set pattern on and off the lead, which includes left turns, right turns, about turns, and changes of pace.
- **Recall:** This may be when the handler is stationary or on the move.
- **Retrieve:** This may be a dumbbell or any article chosen by the judge.
- **Sendaway:** The dog is sent to a designated spot and must go into an instant Down until he is recalled by the handler.
- **Stays:** The dog must stay in the Sit and in the Down for a set amount of time. In advanced classes, the handler is out of sight.
- **Scent:** The dog must retrieve a single cloth from a pre-arranged pattern of cloths that has his owner's scent, or, in advanced classes, the judge's scent. There may also be decoy cloths.
- **Distance control.** The dog must execute a series of moves (Sit, Stand, Down) without moving from his position and with the handler at a distance.

Even though competitive obedience requires accuracy and precision, make it fun for your Cavalier, with lots of praise and rewards, so that you motivate him to do his best. Many training clubs run advanced classes for those who want to compete in obedience, or you can hire the services of a professional trainer for one-on-one sessions.

AGILITY

This fun sport has grown enormously in popularity over the past few years – and Cavaliers love it! If you fancy having a go, make sure you have good control over your Cavalier and keep him slim. Agility is a very physical sport, which demands fitness from both dog and handler. A fat Cavalier is never going to make it as an agility competitor.

In agility competitions, each dog must complete a set course over a series of obstacles, which include:

- Jumps (upright hurdles and long jump)
- Weaves
- A-frame
- Dog walk
- Seesaw
- Tunnels (collapsible and rigid)
- Tyre

Dogs may compete in jumping classes with jumps, tunnels and weaves, or in agility classes, which have the full set of equipment. Faults are awarded for poles down on the jumps, missed contact points on the A-

If you work hard at training and socialising your Cavalier, you will be rewarded with a companion that is second to none.

frame, dog walk and seesaw, and refusals. If a dog takes the wrong course, he is eliminated. The winner is the dog that completes the course in the fastest time with no faults. As you progress up the levels, courses become progressively harder with more twists, turns and changes of direction.

If you want to get involved in agility, you will need to find a club that specialises in the sport (see Appendices). You will not be allowed to start training until your Cavalier is 12 months old, and you cannot compete until he is 18 months old. This rule is for the protection of the dog, who may suffer injury if he puts strain on bones and joints while he is still growing.

DANCING WITH DOGS

This sport is relatively new, but it is becoming increasingly popular. It is very entertaining to watch, but it is certainly not as simple as it looks. To perform a choreographed routine to music with your Cavalier demands a huge amount of training.

Dancing with dogs is divided into two categories: heelwork to music and canine freestyle. In heelwork to music, the dog must work closely with his handler and show a variety of close 'heelwork' positions. In canine freestyle, the routine can be more flamboyant, with the dog working at a distance from the handler and performing spectacular tricks. Routines are judged on style and presentation, content and accuracy.

SUMMING UP

The Cavalier is a brilliant companion dog and is loved the world over. He has an outstanding temperament, and he is fun and rewarding to live with. Make sure you keep your half of the bargain: spend time socialising and training your Cavalier so that you can be proud to take him anywhere and he will always be a credit to you.

THE PERFECT CAVALIER

Chapter 7

So what makes the 'perfect' Cavalier? How do we decide what is, and what is not, a Cavalier King Charles Spaniel? To answer these questions, I need to refer to the Breed Standard, which is the written blueprint describing what a Cavalier King Charles Spaniel should look like.

In the UK, the ruling body for the British dog world is the Kennel Club and one of its key roles is the regulation of all Breed Standards used by judges at Kennel Club licensed shows. These Breed Standards have a uniform layout, with the same clauses in each, ensuring that the important points are covered in order to give a verbal picture of the breed. In the USA, this role is performed by the American Kennel Club.

The FCI (Fédération Cynologique Internationale),

which governs 80 countries throughout Europe and worldwide, has the basic principle that the breed's country of origin determines the Breed Standard. For the Cavalier King Charles Spaniel, the UK has been chosen as the country of origin and, as such, the Breed Standard is virtually identical to the Kennel Club Breed Standard.

HOW IT ALL STARTED

For the Cavalier King Charles Spaniel, we need to thank Mr Roswell Eldridge, an American, who visited Crufts in 1925. He was disappointed that he could find no dogs of the 'old masters' type being shown, so he offered a prize of £25 at Crufts Dog Show in 1926, for the best "old type toy spaniel". As a direct result, a handful of breeders/exhibitors worked together to resurrect the Cavalier King Charles Spaniel. The breed club was founded and,

at the inaugural meeting in 1928, the Standard was drawn up and has remained practically the same from that day to this.

To assist those writing the Breed Standard, a live dog was used, and reproductions of paintings of Toy Spaniels in the sixteenth, seventeenth and eighteenth centuries were referred to, in order to identify the true breed type. The Cavalier King Charles Spaniel in the UK finally achieved Kennel Club status in 1944, following its revival as a breed separate from the King Charles Spaniel.

In the UK, the Cavalier King Charles Spaniel's popularity grew for a variety of reasons, not least because of the breed's happy disposition and ability to adapt to different lifestyles. A Cavalier is equally at home in a grand mansion or in a humble cottage or flat – he is always keen to greet his owners and be given a

News of the Cavalier King Charles Spaniel spread to the USA, and the breed is now well established.

fuss or, better still, set off on an exciting adventure. Eventually, news of the popular Toy Spaniel breed reached America, and the first Cavaliers were exported in 1952.

In 1956 a breed club in America was formed, and enthusiasts sought AKC (American Kennel Club) recognition. But due to the small numbers of Cavaliers in the country, they were relegated to the 'miscellaneous' class in the Toy Group. This led to a formation of a number of breed clubs outside of the auspices of the AKC until, in 1993, the American Cavalier King Charles Spaniel Club was formed. On 1 January 1996 the Cavalier King Charles Spaniel became the

140th AKC recognised breed. A Breed Standard was drawn up, which is naturally based on the KC Standard, but with some important differences, which I have highlighted in my analysis below.

THE PRIORITIES

The Breed Standard gives us a picture of the ideal Cavalier in words. But the 'perfect' dog, in my opinion, has yet to be born. There always seems to be "if only he had that lovely tail-set", or "if only she moved with more drive". But given that more than 90 per cent of all puppies born will go to pet homes, it is essential that custodians of the Breed Standard continue to pay due attention to temperament.

We must ensure that the true Cavalier, who is outgoing, gay, and gentle, is maintained, with no exaggeration in type, keeping true to our forbears' written description of this Toy Spaniel.

Over the years, health issues became a priority. This was the case with heart conditions around 25 years ago – giving the average life-expectancy (from the KC) of a Cavalier at 9.5 yrs – this has now increased to 11.4yrs (as at the survey completed in 2006 by KC). With due attention to all the information around and the help and assistance of the veterinary profession, along with dedicated breeders, we will continue to control and eliminate hereditary diseases and improve the overall health of this popular breed.

PUPPY TO CHAMPION

Breeders are expert at spotting show potential – but there is no such thing as a certainty.

Ricksbury Camilla at Stavonga at seven weeks of age.

Ricksbury Camilla at Stavonga at 14 months.
Russell Fine Art.

Ricksbury Camilla at Stavonga at 10+ years, made up to a Champion.

My perfect dog is one who meets the KC Breed Standard, so that when I read any section I can relate it to my dog, who is balanced, graceful, fearless and gentle, full of breed type, with a happy disposition and outgoing personality; one I can cuddle up to on the sofa as well as hike across the fields with if I am so inclined.

But although the UK is an island, it is not the only place where Cavalier King Charles Spaniels have gained in popularity. Europe, USA and Australia have increasing populations of Cavaliers, and they continue to develop their own Breed Standards broadly based on the KC one, but with emphasis on this and that, with subtle size and point changes, which, if not halted, will begin to change the type over time to evolve into another breed. Remember, there are very few differences between the King Charles and Cavalier King Charles Spaniel.

It is also worth drawing attention to the fact that in 2009, following widespread public concern about the health of pure bred dogs, the Kennel club in the UK introduced the following introductory paragraph to all its Breed Standards:

A Breed Standard is the guideline which describes the ideal characteristics, temperament and appearance of a breed and ensures that the breed is fit for function. Absolute soundness is essential. Breeders and judges should at all times be careful to avoid obvious conditions or exaggerations which would be detrimental in any way to the health, welfare or soundness of this breed. From time to time certain conditions or exaggerations may be considered to have the potential to affect dogs in some breeds adversely, and judges and breeders are requested to refer to the Kennel Club website for details of any such current issues. If a feature or quality is desirable it should only be present in the right measure.

So let us take a look at the KC Breed Standard and its American counterpart, and I will attempt to outline some of the differences as I see them.

INTERPRETING THE BREED STANDARD

GENERAL APPEARANCE

KC
Active, graceful and well balanced, with gentle expression. *Characteristics:* Sporting, affectionate, absolutely fearless. *Temperament:* Gay, friendly non-

We are looking for a graceful, well-balanced Toy spaniel.

The Cavalier is slightly longer in body than he is high.

aggressive, no tendency towards nervousness.

AKC

The Cavalier King Charles Spaniel is an active, graceful, well-balanced toy spaniel, very gay and free in action; fearless and sporting in character, yet at the same time gentle and affectionate. It is this typical gay temperament, combined with true elegance and royal appearance, which are of paramount importance in the breed. Natural appearance with no trimming, sculpting or artificial alteration is essential to breed type.

You will see that the first difference between the KC and the AKC is the general layout and the clubbing together of different points, i.e. General Appearance, Characteristics and Temperament.

Although essentially the Standards are saying the same thing, already there is an emphasis on presentation and 'the look' of the Cavalier. My take on this is that the Cavalier should be able to run or walk for miles, but be equally at home as a household companion with their gentleness and need for companionship. I believe they are as suited to the person in a small flat as one living on a farm – subject to being given sufficient exercise. The Cavalier's hallmark traits are being adaptable, willing to please and biddable.

In terms of general appearance, we are looking for a well-balanced Toy dog between 12 and 18 lbs, slightly longer from withers to tail than from withers to ground, with the tail seen as a continuation of the topline, giving balance and moving happily from side to side. The expression of the Cavalier is

of paramount importance and should be gentle, with soft, melting, dark eyes well set apart with cushioning beneath them. There should be no trace of exaggeration.

HEAD AND SKULL

KC

Skull almost flat between ears. Stop shallow. Length from base of stop to tip of nose about 1 1/2 inches (3.8 cms). Nostrils black and well developed without flesh marks, muzzle well tapered. Lips well developed but not pendulous. Face well filled below eyes. Any tendency to snippiness undesirable.

AKC

Proportionate to size of dog, appearing neither too large nor too small for the body. *Expression:* The sweet, gentle,

The skull should be almost flat between the ears.

Note the subtle differences between the British Cavalier (left) and this American dog.
Photo courtesy: Perkins Creative.

melting expression is an important breed characteristic. *Skull:* Slightly rounded, but without dome or peak; it should appear flat because of the high placement of the ears. Stop is moderate, neither filled nor deep.
Muzzle: Full muzzle slightly tapered. Length from base of stop to tip of nose about 1 1/2 inches. Face well filled below eyes. Any tendency towards snippiness undesirable. Nose pigment uniformly black without flesh marks and nostrils well developed. Lips well developed but not pendulous, giving a clean finish. *Faults:* Sharp or pointed muzzles.

The head should be in proportion to the body with a skull almost flat between the high-set ears that are well feathered. The length of nose (from the base of stop to tip of nose is about 1.5 ins (3.8 cms) with black nostrils, and no flesh-coloured marks. The muzzle should be tapered with the lips, not hound-like but covering the jaw line. A generous head with cushioning beneath the eyes gives the typical gentle expression.

The AKC Standard introduces a few subtle differences, i.e. the KC Breed Standards states: "Skull almost flat between the ears. Stop shallow." The AKC Standard stipulates: "Skull slightly rounded but without dome or peak; it should appear flat because of high placement of the ears. Stop moderate." (The stop is moderate versus shallow in the KC Standard. The look of flatness, according to the AKC Standard, is due to the high placement of ears and not the skull shape.)

I believe breed type is all-important. The head should be well cushioned under the eyes, giving a soft expression, but not over full, which would look out of proportion and coarse. A shallow stop is required as opposed to a deep stop in a King Charles Spaniel, which, when viewed in profile, can appear to be a 90-degree angle. Another undesirable feature for me is hound-like lips.

The lips should not be exaggerated or pendulous, but should just cover the lower jaw.

EYES

KC

Large, dark, round but not prominent; spaced well apart.

AKC

Large, round, but not prominent and set well apart; colour a warm, very dark brown; giving a lustrous, limpid look. Rims dark. There should be cushioning under the eyes which contributes to the soft expression. Faults – Small, almond-shaped, prominent, or light eyes; white surrounding ring.

The Cavalier's unique expression is a soft, melting expression, with large, brown, trusting eyes, which seem to make you the centre of his world.

Here, the AKC Standard emphasises very dark brown eyes versus dark in the KC Breed Standard. It details dark rims, plus the fault of a "white surrounding ring", which is not dealt with in the KC Breed Standard. But, to be fair, this look can give a slightly harsh/pop-eyed look to the Cavalier and is not seen to be desirable by British judges.

EARS

KC

Long, set high, with plenty of feather.

The gentle, melting expression that is so typical of the Cavalier.

AKC

Set high, but not close, on top of the head. Leather long with plenty of feathering and wide enough so that when the dog is alert, the ears fan slightly forward to frame the face.

Again, we see the AKC concentrating on the 'look' of the Cavalier. While the KC Breed Standard wants high-set ears with plenty of feather, the AKC Standard is looking for the ears to "frame the face", and earlier (under Skull) they look to the high-set ears to give the illusion of a flat skull, i.e "should appear flat" rather than looking to the actual structure of the skull, as per the KC Breed Standard.

MOUTH

KC

Jaws strong, with a perfect, regular and complete scissor bite, i.e. the upper teeth closely overlapping the lower teeth and set square to the jaws.

AKC

A perfect, regular and complete scissors bite is

The front legs should be straight and moderately boned.

shoulders to give an elegant look.

Again, in this area, rather than 'moderation', the AKC states "fairly long", which will change the appearance coupled with the other subtle differences. But, hopefully, the judges are reading the whole Breed Standard, and getting a good overall picture, with experience, of what a good Cavalier specimen should look like.

FOREQUARTERS

KC
Chest moderate, shoulders well laid back, straight legs moderately boned.

AKC
Shoulders well laid back. Forelegs straight and well under the dog with elbows close to the sides. Pasterns strong and feet compact with well-cushioned pads. Dewclaws may be removed.

Forelegs should be parallel; no sticking-out elbows or turned-out feet. When the dog moves towards you, the legs should maintain their parallel look, with no pin-toeing or crossing over each other. The shoulders should be well laid back (giving an angle of 90 degrees) so the sternum is evident with plenty of heart room, if viewed from the side. Upright shoulders and a short, steep upper arm will give a hackney-like movement, which is most undesirable.

preferred, i.e. the upper teeth closely overlapping the lower teeth and set square into the jaws. Faults: Undershot bite, weak or crooked teeth, crooked jaws.

Teeth should be even with a scissor bite. A pig or wry mouth (where the lower jaw is twisted to one side, making the jaws out of line with each other) is a fault. Mouths can change in Cavaliers even up to 24 months: a slightly

undershot or level bite, that looks all right in profile as a puppy, may often correct itself.

NECK

KC
Moderate length, slightly arched.

AKC
Fairly long, without throatiness, well enough muscled to form a slight arch at the crest. Set smoothly into nicely sloping

The body is short-coupled and the back is level.

BODY

KC
Short-coupled with good spring of rib. Level back.

AKC
Short-coupled with ribs well sprung but not barrelled. Chest moderately deep, extending to elbows allowing ample heart room. Slightly less body at the flank than at the last rib, but with no tucked-up appearance.

'Short coupled' refers to the length between the last rib and the hip bone. 'Good spring of rib' refers to the rib cage as giving a rounded look, allowing room for the heart and lungs (i.e. not slab sided). The shortness in body is mainly in the lumbar region; this should be well muscled to enable the drive from the hindquarters to propel the dog forward.

HINDQUARTERS

KC
Legs with moderate bone; well turned stifle no tendency to cow or sickle hocks.

AKC
The hindquarters construction should come down from a good broad pelvis, moderately muscled; stifles well turned and hocks well let down. The hind legs when viewed from the rear should parallel each other from hock to heel. Faults – Cow or sickle hocks.

Good hindquarters come down from a broad pelvis (not narrow, which can cause the hind movement being too close). Movement should be parallel. Well-turned stifles are required with good muscle tone on the thighs. The hocks, as seen from the back, should be parallel, with no tendency to being cow hocked, or sickle hocked. Ideally, there should be lots of feathering. Markings should be even on particolours, as uneven markings down the back can give the illusion of poor movement.

The AKC Standard introduces

the term "well let down hocks", which does not appear in the KC Breed Standard. This, again, can change the appearance of the Cavalier King Charles Spaniel. Interestingly enough, British judges have started admiring this feature and putting it in their critiques.

FEET

KC
Compact, cushioned and well feathered.

AKC
See Forequarters and Coat.

Feet are rounded, and well cushioned, with pads and nails of any colour – black spots on a Blenheim are said to show good pigmentation. Exhibitors are allowed to remove excess hair between the pads, but no other trimming is allowed. This can help with hygiene.

TAIL

KC
Length of tail in balance with body, well set on, carried happily but never much above the level of the back. Docking previously optional when no more than one-third was to be removed.

AKC
Well set on, carried happily but

Moderation is the key, and again the Breed Standard calls for hind legs with moderate bone.

never much above the level of the back, and in constant characteristic motion when the dog is in action. Docking is optional. If docked, no more than one third to be removed.

The law regarding the docking of dogs' tails in the UK changed in April 2007. The changes impact the whole of the dog world – from exhibitors and breeders, to judges. Dogs that were docked after this date cannot be shown at any licensed KC event in England and Wales where the general public are admitted, irrespective of whether the docking has been done legally or even in another country.

GAIT/MOVEMENT

KC
Free moving and elegant in action, plenty of drive from behind. Forelegs and hind legs move parallel when viewed from in front and behind.

AKC
Free moving and elegant in action, with good reach in front and sound, driving rear action. When viewed from the side, the movement exhibits a good length of stride, and viewed from front and rear it is straight and true, resulting from straight-boned fronts and properly made and muscled hindquarters.

Correct movement should be elegant, with the dog covering the ground and keeping a level topline in profile; the tail should be an extension of the spine, level with the back or held slightly above. When seen coming towards you or going away from you, the legs fore and hind should move in parallel lines.

COAT

KC
Long, silky, free from curl. Slight wave permissible. Plenty of feathering. Totally free from trimming.

AKC
Of moderate length, silky, free

IN THE RING

The skill of the handler is to catch the judge's eye as the class is assessed.

from curl. **Slight wave permissible. Feathering on ears, chest, legs and tail should be long, and the feathering on the feet is a feature of the breed. No trimming of the dog is permitted. Specimens where the coat has been altered by trimming, clipping, or by artificial means shall be so severely penalized as to be effectively eliminated from competition. Hair growing between the pads on the underside of the feet may be trimmed.**

The long silky coat of the Cavalier is a glamorous feature. In truth, the body coat is only 1.5-2 inches (3.8-5 cms) in length, with generous fringing on the ears, forelegs, on the chest, under the tummy and on the hindquarters, feet and tail. Most coats will begin to look their best from 18 months onwards. The coat should be totally free from trimming.

A slight wave is permissible but curly coats are undesirable. Once a bitch is spayed, the coat becomes coarse and extremely long and profuse (they do not moult every six months with their seasons).

While the KC Breed Standard states "long, silky, free from curl," the AKC Standard states "of moderate length... feathering on ears, chest, legs and tail should be long and the feathering of the feet is a feature of the breed." This is not in the KC Breed Standard. Again, in isolation, it is not a big thing, but, added to the subtle changes in other sections, we are starting to see a change in the 'look' and size of the dog.

COLOURS

KC
Recognised colours are:
• ***Black & Tan:*** **Raven black**

117

with tan markings above the eyes, on cheeks, inside ears, on chest and legs and underside of tail. Tan should be bright. White marks undesirable.

- *Ruby*: Whole coloured rich red. White markings undesirable
- *Blenheim*: Rich chestnut markings well broken up, on pearly white ground. Markings evenly divided on head, leaving room between ears for much valued lozenge mark or spot (a unique characteristic of the breed).
- *Tricolour*: Black and white well spaced, broken up, with tan markings over eyes, cheeks, inside ears, inside legs, and on underside of tail.

Any other colour or combination of colours most undesirable.

AKC

- *Blenheim*: Rich chestnut markings well broken up on a clear, pearly white ground. The ears must be chestnut and the colour evenly spaced on the head and surrounding both eyes, with a white blaze between the eyes and ears, in the centre

White markings are undesirable on whole colours, but mismarked puppies can make great pet dogs.

of which may be the lozenge or "Blenheim spot". The lozenge is a unique and desirable, though not essential, characteristic of the Blenheim.

- *Tricolor*: Jet black markings well broken up on a clear, pearly white ground. The ears must be black and the color evenly spaced on the head and surrounding both eyes, with a white blaze between the eyes. Rich tan markings over the eyes, on cheeks, inside ears and on underside of tail.
- *Ruby*: Whole-coloured rich red.
- *Black and Tan*: Jet black with rich, bright tan markings

over eyes, on cheeks, inside ears, on chest, legs and underside of tail.

Faults – Heavy ticking on Blenheim or Tricolours, white marks on Rubies or Black and Tans.

All colours should have the same silky coat; the particolours should be free from flecking/ticking on the white. Essentially, we are looking for a white dog with large, solid patches of the respective colours, with even markings on the head.

Whole colours should not have any white markings. Occasionally, puppies may have a little white on the toes or chest, or a few hairs on the chin, but this often fades as they grow older and may well disappear before six months.

Basically, both Breed Standards are saying the same with regard to colour/markings and faults in markings, with the AKC Standard listing faults and the KC Standard describing them as 'undesirable'. However, a concern to me is that the AKC chooses to omit a feature of the Cavalier in the tricolour where it only mentions "tan over the eyes, on cheeks, inside ears and on underside of tail". The KC Breed Standard clearly states the

CAVALIER COLOURS

The stunning rich colour of a ruby Cavalier.

Typically, tan markings on a tricolour should be over the eyes, on the cheeks, inside the ears and legs and on the underside of the tail.

Size and weight are becoming increasingly contentious issues in the breed.

addition of tan inside the legs. In the show ring today, you only see around 50 per cent of the tricolours sporting tan on the inside of the legs. Some judges are more forgiving than others on this point, and some judges are more forgiving on a small amount of white on a whole colour.

WEIGHT AND SIZE

KC
Twelve to eighteen pounds (12-18lb/5.4-8.2kg). A small well-balanced dog well within these weights desirable.

AKC
Size: Height 12 to 13 inches at the withers; weight proportionate to height, between 13 and 18 lbs. A small, well balanced dog within these weights is desirable, but these are ideal heights and weights and slight variations are permissible.
Proportion: The body approaches squareness, yet if measured from point of shoulder to point of buttock, is slightly longer than the height at the withers. The height from the withers to the elbow is approximately equal to the height from the elbow to the ground.
Substance: Bone moderate in proportion to size. Weedy and

coarse specimens are to be equally penalized.

The Breed Standard is very much open to personal interpretation, and this is most clearly seen in relation to the section on weight. The KC Standard asks for a dog between 12-18 lbs (5.4-8.2 kgs); this is a tremendous range, even accounting for dogs often being larger than bitches. But interestingly enough, there is only a small percentage of winning dogs today who are not at the top end or, indeed, over the weight quoted. Yet the Breed Standard asks for: "A small well-balanced dog well within these weights desirable". My fear is that if we let this trend continue, we may, at some time in the future, leave the Toy Group. We will change the KC Breed Standard from what it is today, losing the Toy Spaniel we so desire and love, for possibly a sporting spaniel. While I do not advocate dogs meeting the weight criteria prior to being exhibited in all classes, I do feel that due attention needs to be paid to this (one of only two measurements we have in the KC Breed Standard). I feel a minimum is to have a weight class at every Championship Show to encourage awareness of size.

I like to see a well-balanced dog, that is well muscled and meeting the Breed Standard at around 16 lbs (7.26 kgs) with 18 lbs (8.2 kgs) as a maximum. This reduces the size of the dog, and, if the Breed Standard is adhered to with reference to the only other measurement we have – the length of nose from stop to tip – we will have a head in proportion to the body. If this is combined with moderate bone, we are getting a better balanced, graceful dog, naturally free from trimming.

The situation with regard to size is exacerbated by the AKC introducing a measurement for height, which is not included in the KC Standard. The AKC has also decided to change the weight, increasing the minimum by one pound (0.23kg), which is significant in a Toy breed. Again, it refers to the "look" introducing a "squareness" with suggestions on measurement between certain

In the UK, a judge must write a critique on his first and second placed dogs.

points, with details of what type(s) should be penalised.

FAULTS

KC
Any departure from the foregoing points should be considered a fault and the seriousness with which the fault should be regarded should be in exact proportion to its degree and its effect upon the health and welfare of the dog. Note: Male animals should have two apparently normal testicles fully descended into the scrotum.

AKC
See listings under various headings throughout.

Last and by no means least, when discussing 'faults' the KC Breed Standard allows the judge to judge the whole animal and make an assessment against where that animal stacks up against the Breed Standard –

remember, the perfect dog has yet to be bred. However, the AKC Breed Standard states "Bad temper, shyness and meanness are not to be tolerated and are to be so severely penalized as to effectively remove the specimen from competition." So perhaps a little prescriptive and maybe a little, dare I say, over zealous.

In the UK, following a judging appointment, the judge is required to write a critique on the first and second winners at Championships shows, which is published in the two main dog papers. The critique enables the exhibitor to see the dog through the judge's eyes on the day, and helps those wanting to have a better understanding of their dog, as perceived by the judge, against the Breed Standard – which is what we should all be working towards. However, in the AKC system there is no need for the judge to write a critique – a missed opportunity to educate the exhibitor and reinforce the Breed Standard, in my opinion.

It is our duty to promote Cavaliers that remain true to the intentions of the pioneers who developed the breed.

SUMMING UP

As we have seen, there are a number of small but significant differences between the KC Breed Standard, which is based on the 'ideal' as perceived by the pioneers of the breed in the UK, and the AKC Breed Standard, drawn up so many years later.

The AKC has chosen to add some measurements, raising the lower weight measurement, introducing a height measurement and putting a different slant on the Breed Standard in some minor aspects, such as the shape of the head/skull, markings on the tricolour, and making the feathering on the feet a feature. This, in my opinion, is changing the Breed Standard, and the subtle differences are crossing the Atlantic and impacting on the interpretation of the KC Breed Standard in the UK.

Many opinions have been expressed as to why this might be, but I believe that it is based on purely commercial considerations. Many Cavaliers are exported to the USA every year, and the USA is by far the largest importer of Cavaliers from the UK. It would therefore be unrealistic not to expect British breeders to take note of differences in the AKC Breed Standard, and choose, on some occasions, to incorporate them into their breeding programme. More British breeders are producing dogs for the US market, and often when US judges officiate in the UK, they put up Cavaliers of the type they are used to seeing in their own country (as opposed to our KC Breed Standard). This is despite the fact that when a judge officiates in a foreign country, he should judge according to that country's ruling body's Breed Standard.

I fear that if the changes I have highlighted in the American Breed Standard were to continue unchecked, we could be in danger of creating another breed. If you look at the Cocker Spaniel and the American Cocker Spaniel, they are two distinct breeds – yet they started off the same breed until the AKC made changes. Are the changes referred to above the thin edge of the wedge? Will we end up having two different breeds in years to come? Only time will tell.

The FCI is a collection of 80 countries with wide differences in their traditions of purebred dogs. The skill and knowledge in drawing up Breed Standards that can stand the test of time and avoid addressing passing fashions and fads can be equally variable. Sometimes politics can play a part in determining the 'Country of Origin' (i.e. a breed may have originated from one country but if, when it was approved by the FCI, the numbers of that breed were greater in another country, the FCI may approve the other country's Breed Standard rather than that of the originating country). However, we shall leave that debate for another time. Suffice to say, with respect to our breed, the FCI chose the KC (UK) Breed Standard, which I believe was the right and only

Remember, win or lose, the best dog is the one you take home with you...

choice. Incidentally, the FCI goes further with critique writing in some countries and insists that a critique be written for every dog exhibited. This was a challenge to me the first time I completed an assignment under FCI regulations in France, but I found it concentrated the mind on referring to the Breed Standard, and, as an exhibitor, I would find it very helpful.

HAPPY AND HEALTHY

8

Chapter

Most dogs enjoy life if they are fit, healthy and well exercised. Cavalier King Charles Spaniels have especially active minds and respond well to new situations. In order to keep your Cavalier King Charles Spaniel fit, you must provide him with opportunities for stimulating walks to provide interest, as well as taking care of his physical health with the correct diet and the necessary vaccinations and parasite control.

Visits to the veterinary surgeon will be required for vaccinations, at which time it is usual to make a physical examination of the dog for any undisclosed disease. In between times, daily grooming provides the opportunity to get to know the dog's body structure and coat, so that signs of illness can be detected early. The introduction of improved,

balanced diets and routine vaccinations are contributing to a much longer life for all domestic animals, but the owner also has a role to play in everyday health care.

It is very important that you really get to know your dog, as you will more easily identify when the dog is 'off colour'. You should then be able to decide whether the dog needs to be rested or taken to the veterinary surgery. It is also important to know the signs of a healthy dog when you go to buy a puppy. Visits to the vet should be made soon after acquiring your Cavalier, where any abnormalities may be detected. Pet insurance cover has provided the opportunity for extensive tests and procedures to be undertaken on dogs. You should always find out what each policy will offer and if there are limits put on total claim expense, age limit or hereditary disorders

requiring veterinary attention before purchasing insurance.

VACCINATIONS
It is best to take all available measures to keep your Cavalier healthy; one of the greatest advances in canine practice in the last 50 years has been the development of effective vaccines to prevent diseases. Within living memory, dogs died from fits after distemper virus infections and in the last 20 years many puppies have contracted the potentially fatal parvovirus. The routine use of a multiple component vaccine to protect against canine distemper, infectious canine hepatitis, parvovirus and Leptospirosis is accepted, but there are still local differences in the age the puppy receives his first injection or 'shot'. The timing for the primary vaccine course dose is based on an understanding of when the

A puppy needs to be protected against infectious diseases that can be lethal.

immunity provided by the mother declines to a level that will not interfere with the immune response. Canine vaccines currently in use in the UK have recommendations for the final dose of the primary course to be given at 10 or 12 weeks of age, with annual booster injections after the first year.

The length of protection given to a puppy after two injections against Leptospirosis is not significantly greater than 12 months (challenges after this date results in shedding of Leptospires), and for some vaccines it is considered less than 12 months. For the protection against the dog viruses, a minimum of three years is possible and here annual boosters are less essential. In the way of

natural things, not all dogs would be protected, so further booster vaccination is recommended at intervals. This should be decided by your vet, with a local knowledge, to protect any dogs who may have low or marginal blood-level immunity against fatal diseases.

Kennel cough is a distressing, infectious disease, usually acquired from airborne contact with other dogs, especially those stressed when visiting dog shows or boarding kennels. There are several vaccines available and again advice should be obtained from the vet as to which type of protection is appropriate for your dog. The rabies vaccine is necessary for all dogs leaving the United Kingdom, but is routine in many countries, as is the

vaccine for Lyme disease in the USA, where it should be discussed with the veterinarian. Coronavirus, a cause of diarrhoea, is not life-threatening and vaccination is not usually considered necessary.

WORMING AND PARASITE CONTROL

Routine worming every three months is obligatory to reduce the risk of infection of susceptible humans handling the dog. De-wormers are necessary for puppies as well as for adult dogs. Many puppies are infested with roundworms, but some breeders start worming the bitch whilst pregnant to reduce the risk to the newborn pups. Worming of the puppy from two weeks, repeated at regular intervals, is advised.

Roundworms, hookworms, tapeworms and whipworms present different threats, while heartworms, which can result after the bite of an infected mosquito, are a particular problem in the south-east Atlantic and Gulf coasts of the USA. This is another parasite to consider if you are planning to take your dog to mainland Europe, as heartworm is endemic in the Mediterranean area of France.

Fleas are wingless insects that are a nuisance to pets. A single flea on the dog's coat can cause persistent scratching and restlessness. Even after the flea has been removed the bites can cause skin disease, particularly if there is hypersensitivity to flea antigen. Fleas may also carry the larvae of the worm Dipylidium, which causes tapeworms to develop in the host's intestine when the flea is swallowed by a dog, cat or even a child. Many effective anti-flea preparations are now available – some as tablets by mouth, some as coat applications and some as residual sprays to apply to carpets and upholstery frequented by cats as well as dogs.

Lice, fleas, Cheyletiella and other mites that burrow under the skin or on the surface are not easily recognised by the eye and may all cause disease. Ticks become visible as they gorge themselves with the dog's blood. A thorough grooming of the dog each day will help to detect many of these parasites, which can then be prevented using

Routine treatment is needed to prevent infestation from fleas.

products as needed. These may be supplied as a powder, a shampoo, a spot-on insecticide or spray.

DIET AND EXERCISE FOR HEALTH

Many Cavaliers are naturally lean and are perfectly fit, even though they appear to carry little body fat. It is a good idea to weigh all dogs on a regular basis; dogs that appear thin but are still actively fit have fewer reserves to fall back on, and weighing on a weekly basis can detect further weight loss before any disastrous changes can occur. Each dog should have an ideal weight, and within a narrow range the actual correct weight for the dog will act as a guide.

Obesity has become a major concern for dogs as well as

A gleaming coat is a good indicator of a dog's health and wellbeing.

humans. Appetite suppressants for dogs can now be used; mitratapide is available from the vet and can be used as part of an overall weight management programme.

COAT, EARS AND FEET

A Cavalier's coat should not be short, but of moderate length and silky. Too much indoor confinement, with warm room temperatures, can lead to loss of undercoat and less hair density for outdoor protection.

Regular grooming stimulates the hair growth stage known as anagen, by the removal of dead, shedding hairs. This helps to prevent bareness or bald patches. The removal of any eye or other discharge prevents coat matting and skin irritation. The close inspection of the animal during grooming assists in the early recognition of problems.

During grooming, daily care and attention to bony prominences, skin folds, feet and claws, eyes and ears, mouth and teeth, anus, vulva and prepuce contributes to the health of the dog. Regular checks for traces of fleas or ticks attached to the skin can prevent itching and hair loss. When grooming the dog, always make a point of checking the ears, both inside and out. There may often be a slightly sweet smell, but as soon as ear problems occur, the aroma becomes very pungent. The start of ear trouble can be detected by observing the way the dog holds his head and the presence of an unpleasant odour. You may need to wash the Cavalier King Charles Spaniel's coat, either to eradicate and control ectoparasites or to cleanse the coat and remove smells. Bathing is also used to improve the appearance of the coat before a show.

The pads of the feet should feel quite soft to touch and not leathery or horny (hyperkeratinised). The skin between the toes is very sensitive to chemical burns, and some alkaline clay soils will provoke inflammation with lameness known as 'pedal eczema'. The nails should be of even length and not split at the ends, after being left to grow too long. If the nails are too long, they will have to be clipped, being especially careful to avoid cutting into the quick. Exercise on hard concrete surfaces and pavements is normally sufficient to keep nails at a reasonable length; tarmac roads and tarred pavements do not often provide enough friction to wear down nails. Dewclaws are not a disadvantage to the dog, but if they grow in a circle, they can penetrate the flesh, causing an infected wound.

A TO Z OF COMMON AILMENTS

ALLERGIES

Allergies are now a frequent diagnosis for many dog skin and intestinal disorders, and are the result of an inappropriate immune response by the dog to an antigen in the food or to one inhaled through the nose. Unfortunately, there are many antigens that can affect dogs, and diagnostic skin and blood tests may not always identify the disease factor. A process of eliminating possible antigens in the diet or in the environment may help to find a cause, and there are many commercial diets available that can be useful. Medication can be used to suppress the allergic response and both antihistamines and steroids may be tried before the best treatment is found.

ALOPECIA

This is the partial or complete absence of hair from areas of the skin where it is normally present; it is often first seen as a patchy coat loss. This disorder is usually hormonal, associated with hypothyroidism, hyperadrenocorticism (Cushing's disease), sertoli cell tumour of the testes, or, in females, an ovarian imbalance of the hormones. Hair loss may occur after animal bites, but when the hair loss is on both sides of the body (often on the flanks) and the skin is not itchy or inflamed, alopecia may be the cause. Treatment must first be based on identifying and treating the underlying cause. Lotions applied direct to the skin will not cure the problem, but moisturising creams will reduce scaliness.

A process of elimination is often required to discover the cause of an allergy.

Arthritis is more likely to affect an older dog.

ANAEMIA

This is a blood condition, where there is not enough haemoglobin in the blood to carry oxygen, or where there are insufficient red blood cells. Anaemia can only be diagnosed after the examination of a sample of the dog's blood. Veterinary examinations involving blood tests will help find the cause of the anaemia and the most appropriate treatment.

ANAL DISORDERS

Modern diets are often blamed for the frequency of dogs needing their anal glands squeezed out at regular intervals. These glands are actually little sacs just at the edge of the anus opening and contain strong-smelling, greasy substances, used to 'mark' the freshly passed faeces for other animals to recognise. Over-production of the fluid causes the dog discomfort, and, when a suitable floor surface is available, the dog will then 'scoot' along, leaving a trail of odorous matter. Occasionally, infection alters the smell and may result in other dogs being attracted to a female

type odour; a course of antibiotics can be beneficial.

Abscesses of the anal sacs are very painful. They may require drainage, although often they swell and burst on their own with a sudden blood-stained discharge. Antibiotics may be required as treatment.

Other glands around the anus may become cancerous and attention is drawn to these when bleeding occurs. Adenomata are found in the older male dog and require veterinary attention before bleeding occurs.

ARTHRITIS

Arthritis was once a joint disease that was often found after an infection, but now it is usually either due to joint wear and tear (degenerative) or as a result of the immune system reaction, such as rheumatoid arthritis and idiopathic arthritis. Treatment is aimed at keeping the dog mobile; excess weight should be lost and anti-inflammatory medication on a daily basis will remove pain and discomfort.

ATOPY

Sometimes known as inhalant allergy, this is associated with many chronic skin diseases characterised by pruritus (itching). This is a sensation within the skin that provokes the Cavalier to have a desire to scratch, lick, chew or rub himself to alleviate the irritation. It is not as common in the Cavalier as in some dog breeds, but may require specific tests and medication to relieve the itching. The signs do not usually develop until one to three years and is characterised by roughened, itchy, oozing skin, caused by the immune reactions to various allergens, such as fleas or pollen. There is an indication of an inherited tendency, as some breeds are more susceptible, and there is often a seasonal change if specific pollens are the cause. (See Inherited Disorders.)

BENIGN TUMOURS

Benign tumours are cancers that do not invade the body aggressively, but appear as

BRONCHITIS

Inflammation of the breathing tubes is often the result of a virus or a bacterial infection, but irritant gases and dust can also be the cause of repeated coughing. Kennel cough is the most common infection, which results in sticky mucus clinging to the base of the windpipe (trachea) and the tubes entering the lungs (bronchii). Coughing similar to bronchitis is seen in older dogs, associated with congestive heart failure, which may occur with a failing heart muscle and fluid accumulating in the lungs.

Antibiotics may be prescribed by the vet, to reduce the bronchitis signs and the risk of further bacterial infection leading to generalised pneumonia. Cough suppressants and 'antitussives' can be used to suppress a persistent cough, but should not be used if there is bronchopneumonia.

swellings or lumps, often detected during the grooming process. They can cause problems if they grow large, such as a lipoma in the armpit (axilla), or if they are in a position where they can get knocked or bleed after scratching. Most warts are benign growths, but they have to be distinguished from mast cell tumours, which occur on the skin of the body, especially the lower abdomen and hind legs, and may be life-threatening. Growths may be present for months or years before suddenly enlarging. Where there is any doubt, a biopsy test should be taken and surgical excision may be called for.

BURNS AND SCALDS

First-aid measures require immediate cooling of the skin by pouring cold water over the burn or scald repeatedly for at least 10 minutes. Some scalds, from spilt hot water or oil, will penetrate the coat and may not be seen until a large area of skin and hair peels away, due to the heat killing the surface skin cells. As these injuries are considered to be very painful, analgesics (pain relief) should be obtained from the vet, and in anything but the smallest injured area, antibiotics are advisable, as secondary bacteria will multiply on exposed, raw surfaces. Bandages and dressings are not a great help, but clingfilm

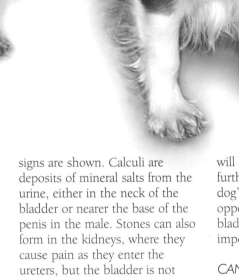

The responsible owner should learn the principles of first aid.

has been used as a protective layer in some situations. Clipping the hair away over a large area surrounding the burn and then flushing with saline may be tolerated by the dog. An Elizabethan collar can be used to prevent the Cavalier licking the area. In cases where the dog is showing signs of shock, intravenous fluid therapy may be necessary.

CALCULI

Stones were often thought to be the cause of a dog straining to pass urine, and a veterinary examination for bladder inflammation (cystitis) or tumours is advised where these signs are shown. Calculi are deposits of mineral salts from the urine, either in the neck of the bladder or nearer the base of the penis in the male. Stones can also form in the kidneys, where they cause pain as they enter the ureters, but the bladder is not affected.

Calculi are recognisable on X-ray or with ultrasound examinations. The obstruction may be partial, when the dog or bitch spends an unusually long time passing urine, or in males, sometimes no urine can be voided and the dog strains, looking uncomfortable or in pain. An operation is usually necessary to remove calculi and diet advice will be given on how to avoid further attacks. Increasing the dog's water intake and providing opportunities for frequent bladder emptying are equally important in prevention.

CANCER – CARCINOMA

The frequency of cancer in Cavaliers is no greater than any other breed, but as dogs are now living longer, it may seem that more owners will have a dog affected by cancerous tumours, often in the dog's later years. One in every four dogs is likely to have one of the many types of cancer. Carcinoma may be seen as an abnormal swelling or 'growth', but internal tumours will not be recognised so readily. Bleeding from the mouth, nose or rectum should always arouse fears of a tumour. Skin tumours may first be noticed as sores that will not heal or raised areas with a tendency to bleed.

Sarcomas are malignant tumours arising from the connective tissues; one of the commonest forms is lymphosarcoma, a tumour of the lymph tissues. Mammary tumours are probably the most common cancers of the bitch, but they are rarely found in females spayed before their second season. About 50 per cent of such tumours in the dog are benign, but mixed tumours may occur and removal of affected glands is usually advised. The earlier a tumour is found, the better.

The vet may need to X-ray or take cell samples known as biopsies. Treatment will depend on the result of such tests. Surgical excision may be the first treatment applied, but other tumours respond to chemotherapy or radiotherapy. Freezing, using cryotherapy, is one of many treatments that may be appropriate for a certain type of growth, and tumours appear to be completely removed by this procedure. Palliative surgery may be used to remove a tumour to improve the animal's quality of life, even though it does not alter the long-term prognosis.

CARDIAC DISORDERS

Heart disease may show itself in many forms. Young puppies may have abnormal heart sounds and a congenital heart defect, but cardiac problems are more common in the older Cavalier. Medication has improved tremendously in recent years and can give a good long-term prognosis. There are many conditions of the heart valves and blood vessels, but one of the most common is the weakening of the heart muscle known as myocardial degeneration. Dilated cardiomyopathy (DM) is a problem in many dog breeds. The heart has some capacity to compensate for disease, but, when exceeded, the heart fails. The signs of blood congestion are: weakness, coughing, loss of appetite and a disinclination to go for walks. A rapid heart beat with a weak pulse, pale or bluish lips and gums, a swollen stomach (ascites) are signs to watch for. Syncope is the condition reached when the dog collapses; emergency treatment with oxygen and ensured rest should accompany appropriate heart medication.

Cavaliers, both young and old, may suffer with mild to severe heart valve problems, but careful control of exercise and diet can help to maintain a comfortable old age. One of the most common forms is mitral valve defect, leading to heart failure. This is seen as a shortness of breath and body swellings due to the retention of sodium and water. Coughing, tiredness, weakness and sudden death can

Remember to deduct treats from the daily food ration in order to maintain the correct weight.

occur. Supplements to help the heart muscle may be used – carnitine, arginine and taurine help, together with the restriction of dietary sodium. A lowering of the dog's salt intake should take place over five days, allowing time for the kidneys to adjust. Some dogs lose their appetite, resulting in weight loss; special diets containing easily digestible energy food and fat to increase palatability may be used in heart disorders. (See Inherited Disorders.)

COLLAPSE

Sudden collapse and possible loss of consciousness is associated with any sudden pain or possibly poisoning in young, working dogs. If seen in old age, it is more likely to be due to heart or circulatory failure. Ensuring that the dog has a clear airway for breathing and massaging the chest area may be all that can be done until the dog gets to a vet, where a full examination will be necessary.

CONSTIPATION

If your Cavalier has consumed large quantities of bone or fibrous matter, straining may indicate a foreign body stuck in the rectum or, in the male dog, it may be due to an enlarged prostate gland. Treatment with liquid paraffin and increasing the fluid intake is advised, but if the problem continues, veterinary advice should be sought.

CYSTITIS

Inflammation of the bladder is more common in the female and may first be noticed by the bitch

CATARACTS

Any opaqueness of the lens of the eye is termed a cataract. The dog may be blind, and the eye has a 'pearl-like' quality to it. Cataracts are most commonly seen in old age or in dogs with diabetes, but they can occur in young dogs, following an injury (such as a thorn piercing the eye). Some breeds are affected with congenital cataracts, which is seen once the puppy opens its eyes. Once the condition has been diagnosed, cataract surgery performed at specialised ophthalmic centres is very successful. (See Inherited Disorders.)

straining frequently, with only small quantities of urine passed each time. Bacteria reaching the bladder from outside the body is the usual cause, although bladder calculi are fairly common in both sexes and will also cause cystitis. In all cases, the fluid intake should be reviewed, since a good 'wash through' of the bladder will reduce the risk of bacteria and mineral particles irritating the bladder lining. Medication with antispasmodics and an appropriate antibiotic will be required.

DIABETES

One of the two sorts found in the dog, 'sugar diabetes' (known as DM – diabetes mellitus), is seen more frequently in the older bitch and is caused by a lack of insulin to regulate the level of glucose in the blood. The signs of increased thirst, passing large

quantities of urine, eye cataracts and muscle weakness are seen alongside an increased appetite and weight loss, as the dog attempts to satisfy the variations of his sugar levels. Diagnosis by urine and blood samples is followed by a regular injection of a suitable insulin under the skin, once or more daily. Some types of endocrine disease, such as diabetes, may arise as a result of an immune-mediated destruction of glandular tissues.

It is now possible to monitor the dog's glucose level through a sensor that samples every two hours. This may be used in dogs that are difficult to stabilise on injected insulin.

The other type of diabetes – diabetes insipidus – is related to the water control mechanism of the kidneys and is uncommon in dogs.

DISTEMPER

Fortunately, this virus infection, which at one time caused devastating illnesses, is now rare. Routine vaccination has been very effective in preventing disease, but there is always the threat of a Cavalier acquiring the infection if there has been a breakdown in the immune system. Affected dogs develop a high temperature, cough, diarrhoea and a purulent eye

The Cavalier has large eyes, which can make him prone to conditions such as conjunctivitis.

discharge; then, after several weeks, illness complications may still set in with pneumonia or damage to the nervous system, seen as paralysis or fits.

EYE PROBLEMS

Conjunctivitis is common in dogs with prominent eyes; the signs of a red eye, with a watery or crusty discharge, are easy to recognise. Dust blown by the wind, chemicals and allergies cause eye irritation, but sudden, acute, severe conjunctivitis may indicate the presence of a foreign body, such as a grass seed, under the eyelid. Careful examination of the inner surfaces of both eyelids and the third eyelid is necessary to identify and remove foreign material. Another cause is the in-turning of the edge of the eyelid, known as entropion; it is sometimes inherited and surgical correction may be required.

There are other eye disorders, such as corneal dystrophy, ulcers, keratitis, or a 'dry eye' (KCS), which all require specific veterinary attention. (See Inherited Disorders.)

EPILEPSY AND FITS

Seizures occur relatively commonly in dogs. They represent an acute and usually brief disturbance of normal electrical activity in the brain,

A change in diet may cause a digestive upset.

but can be distressing for both the patient and the owner. Most fits last only a short time (less than two minutes) and owners often telephone for veterinary advice once the seizure is over. Fits can sometimes occur close together, and it is best to have the animal examined by a veterinary surgeon as soon as possible, even after the seizure has stopped. Some fits are prolonged or very frequent, and such seizures may cause permanent brain damage. Once the fits have passed, the dog may seem dull or confused for several hours. Medication is used to control fits but long-term treatment may be needed. Screaming when touched may be due to syringomyelia. (See Inherited Disorders.)

FRACTURES

Most broken bones are the result of some avoidable injury; an old dog with kidney disease may have brittle bones, but spontaneous fractures are quite rare even then. Treatment of fractures will require the attention of the vet, but there is little point in attempting first-aid, as the Cavalier will be in pain and will adopt the most comfortable position possible. Natural painkillers known as endorphins come into action immediately following such an injury. If there is a skin wound associated with the fracture, this should be covered to reduce bacterial contamination, reducing the risk of osteomyelitis before the break in the bone can be satisfactorily repaired. X-rays will be necessary to confirm a crack or a major displacement of bones.

GASTRO-ENTERITIS

Vomiting is relatively common in dogs and can be a protective mechanism, to try to prevent poisonous substances entering the body. Gastro-enteritis includes diarrhoea attacks, as a similar process to get rid of undesirable intestine contents by washing them out. The production of extra mucus and intestinal fluid, coupled with a rapid bowel evacuation movement, accounts for the large volumes of slimy faeces. These products of gastro-enteritis are distressing to the dog and unpleasant for the owner who may have to clean up afterwards. There are many causes, ranging from the dog simply needing worming, to the complex interaction of viruses and bacteria that can cause an infection to spread through a kennel. Dietary diarrhoea may occur after a sudden change in foodstuff, after scavenging (a packet of butter is stolen, for example), or due to an allergy to a particular food substance or an additive. Where the signs of gastro-enteritis last more than 48 hours, a vet should be prepared to take samples and other tests to look for diseases such as pancreatitis, colitis or tumours, since some disorders may be life-threatening.

Treatment at home should consist of 'bowel rest', where the owner stops feeding for 48 to 72 hours; fluids are allowed in repeated small quantities. Ice cubes in place of water in the bowl may help reduce vomiting. Electrolyte solutions help with rehydration. Once signs are alleviated, small feeds of smooth foods (such as steamed fish or chicken and boiled rice) may be gradually introduced. Where there is continual diarrhoea for three to four weeks, the disease is unlikely to resolve without a specific cause being identified and treated appropriately by the vet.

HEARTWORM DISEASE

Heartworms are still uncommon in the UK, but are a major problem in the USA, where they are spread by mosquitoes. Dogs can be protected from six to eight weeks of age, with a monthly dose of the medication advised by the veterinarian. A blood test can be used to see if the heartworm antigen is present

before commencing treatment and it can be repeated annually. The filarial worms live in the heart and blood vessels of the lungs and cause signs such as tiredness, intolerance of exercise and a soft, deep cough.

HEPATITIS

Inflammation of the liver may be due to a virus, but it is uncommon in dogs when they have been vaccinated against the bacteria Leptospira from damaging the liver. Chronic liver disease may be due to heart failure, tumours or some type of toxicity; dietary treatment may help if no specific medicines are prescribed.

JAUNDICE

The yellow colour of the skin, most noticeably seen in the white of the eye, is a sign of liver

damage and retention of the yellow pigment from the breakdown of blood haemoglobin. Jaundice is usually accompanied by a loss of appetite and general disinterest in exercise, since the liver is a key organ in the dog's body system controls. Veterinary attention is urgent since adequate treatment can make jaundice disappear over a few weeks. Care must be taken to avoid further liver damage and some dogs may become carriers of infection (see Leptospirosis.)

KENNEL COUGH

The signs of a goose-honking cough, hacking or retching that lasts from a few days to several weeks are due to cell damage at the base of the windpipe and bronchial tubes. The dry and unproductive cough is caused by

Kennel cough will spread rapidly among dogs that live together.

LYME DISEASE BORRELIOSIS

This tick-borne disease affecting dogs, humans and, to a lesser extent, other domestic animals is common in the USA; it is estimated that there may be a thousand cases a year in the UK. Often there will be sudden lameness with a fever or, in the chronic form, one or two joints are affected with arthritis, often in the carpus (wrist joint), which alerts the Cavalier owner to this disease. Exposure to ticks (Ixodes ricinus in Britain) should raise suspicions if similar signs develop with swelling of a joint and loss of appetite, especially if a rash develops at the bite, which soon spreads. Treatment is effective and blood tests can be used to confirm Borrelia at the laboratory.

a combination of viruses, bacteria and mycoplasma. Vaccination is helpful in preventing the disease, but may not give full protection, as strains of kennel cough seem to vary. The disease is highly contagious and spread by droplets, so it may be acquired at dog shows or boarding kennels. An incubation period of five to seven days is usual. Veterinary treatments alleviate the cough and reduce the duration of the illness.

LEPTOSPIROSIS

Dogs that work in the country or swim in water may be more likely to contract this infection. Leptospira bacteria carried by rats may be found in pools and ditches where rodents have visited. Annual vaccination against the two types of Leptospira is advised. Antibiotic treatment in the early stages is effective, but liver and kidney damage may permanently incapacitate the Cavalier if the early signs, with a fever, are not recognised. Kidney and liver failure may lead to death. Treatment with antibiotics for two to three weeks is needed to prevent the dog carrying Leptospira and infecting others.

MANGE MITES

Several types affecting dogs are recognised and may be the cause of scratching, hair loss and ear disease. Sarcoptic mange causes the most irritation and is diagnosed by skin scrapings or a blood test. Demodectic mange is less of a problem and is diagnosed by skin scrapes or from plucked hairs. Otodectic mange occurs in the ears and the mite can be found in the wax. Cheyletiella is a surface mite of the coat; it causes white 'dandruff' and is diagnosed by coat brushings or sellotape impressions for microscope inspection. These mite infections first need identifying, but can then be treated with acaracide medication provided by the vet. Older, traditional treatments required frequent bathing of the dog. Repeat treatments after 10 to 14 days are needed to prevent re-infestation

NEPHRITIS

Dogs may suffer acute kidney failure after poisoning, obstructions to the bladder or after shock with reduced blood supply. Chronic nephritis is more common in older dogs, where the blood accumulates waste products that the damaged kidneys cannot remove. The nephritic syndrome is caused by immune-mediated damage within the kidney. The signs of increased thirst, loss of appetite and progressive weight loss are commonly seen in kidney disease.

OTITIS EXTERNA

Ear diseases are more common in dogs, such as the Cavalier, that have drop-down ear flaps. When there is a lot of hair around the ear, the ventilation of the tube to the ear drum is poor and may encourage bacteria to multiply. When otitis occurs, a

The Cavalier has long drop-down ear flaps, and so may be prone to ear infections.

strong-smelling discharge develops and the dog shakes his head or may show a head tilt. The presence of a grass seed in the ear canal should always be suspected in dogs that have been out in long grass in the summer months; after becoming trapped by the hair, the seed can quickly work its way down the ear canal and even penetrate the ear drum. The spikes of the grass seed prevent it being shaken out of the ear and veterinary extraction of the seed is essential.

PARALYSIS AND INTERVERTEBRAL DISC DISEASE

Collapse or sudden weakness of the hindquarters may be due to pressure on the nerves of the spine that supply the muscles and other sensory receptors. The 'slipped disc', as it is commonly known, may be responsible, but any injury to the spine – a fibrocartilage embolism, a fracture or a tumour – may cause similar paralysis. The signs are similar, with the dog dragging one or both hind legs,

lack of tail use and often the loss of bladder and bowel control. X-rays, a neurological assessment and possibly an MRI scan will be needed to be certain of the cause. Some cases respond well to surgical correction, but others are effectively treated by medicines, which are less costly. Home nursing care should keep the dog clean and groomed, help with bladder or bowel movement, and implement physiotherapy exercises advised by the veterinary surgeon. Sudden movements in the case of

A bitch who has been neutered is free from the risk of pyometra.

Medication to stop the vomiting, antibiotics against secondary bacteria, and later a smooth, bland diet may be provided.

PROSTATE DISEASE

Elderly dogs that have not been castrated may show signs of straining, which can be thought to be a sign of constipation, but an enlarged prostate gland at the neck of the bladder will often be the real cause. Most often it is a benign enlargement that causes pressure in the rectum, rather than blocking the bladder exit. Once diagnosed, hormone injections combined with a laxative diet can be very effective.

PYOMETRA

At one time, this was the commonest cause of illness in middle-aged to elderly bitches. The disease of the uterus would be seen in both bitches never bred from and those who had litters earlier in life. The cause is an imbalance of the hormones that prepare the lining of the uterus for puppies, so that fluid and mucus accumulates. This leads to an acute illness if bacteria invade the organ. 'Open pyometra' is when a blood-stained mucoid discharge comes out, often sticking to the hairs around the vulva; it has been confused with a bitch coming on heat unexpectedly. It can be more difficult to diagnose the cause of illness when there is no discharge present, this is known as a 'closed pyometra'; other ways of testing the patient for the uterus disorder may be employed by

spinal fractures must be avoided when carrying a patient with any back injury.

PARVOVIRUS

The virus infection of younger dogs is most dangerous to the recently weaned puppy. Vaccination schedules are devised to protect susceptible dogs and the vet should be asked as to

how often a parvo vaccine should be used in your locality. The virus has an incubation of about three to five days. It attacks the bowels with sudden-onset vomiting and diarrhoea. Blood may be passed, dehydration sets in and sudden death is possible. Isolation from other puppies is essential; replacement of the fluids and electrolytes lost is urgent.

your vet. Although medical treatments are available, it is more usual to perform a hysterectomy, especially if the bitch has come to the end of her breeding career.

RABIES

This fatal virus infection is almost unknown in the UK, but it remains as a cause of death of animals and humans in parts of the world where preventive vaccine is not in regular use. The disease attacks a dog's central nervous system and is spread by infective saliva, usually following after the bite of an animal developing the disease. Annual rabies vaccination is an important way of controlling the disease.

RINGWORM

Ringworm is a fungus disease of the skin that has nothing to do with worms, but it acquired the name from the circular red marks on the skin following infection. It may appear as bald, scaly patches and will spread to children or adults handling the dog unless precautions are taken. Treatments will vary depending on the extent of the problem: the vet can advise painting a small area with povidone-iodine repeatedly, or an all-over wash with a fungicide, applied every three days, can be effective. Another method is to dose the dog with Griseofulvin tablets for three to four weeks; it should not be used in pregnancy – of a bitch or a handler.

VESTIBULAR DISEASE

Older Cavaliers may develop a head tilt, often with eye-flicking movements known as nystagmus. At one time, this was commonly diagnosed as a 'stroke' because of its suddenness; the dog may circle or fall on one side, rolling, as the dog cannot balance itself. Vestibular disease develops suddenly, but unlike the equivalent human stroke, there is no sign of bleeding nor of a vascular accident in the brain. Recovery is slow and the brain regains its balance centre after one to three weeks. Treatment by the vet will assist a return to normal, although some dogs always carry their head with a tilt. Where the head tilt persists or signs get worse, a specialist investigation may be needed to detect an inner ear disease infection or a brain tumour.

INHERITED DISORDERS

Healthy parents for breeding puppies should always be selected. Responsible breeders of Cavalier King Charles Spaniels have done much to improve the breed and eliminate undesirable features.

ATOPIC DERMATITIS

Signs of this condition are roughened, itchy skin caused by an immune system disease and it is thought there is a hereditary basis. It is not a major breed problem but may occur in some Cavaliers.

EYE CONDITIONS

Cataracts are found in the breed and may be inherited. They may take the form of congenital lens opacity, which can be recognised

It is essential that all potential breeding stock is cleared of inherited disorders.

HEART AND MITRAL VALVE DISEASE

Chronic heart valve disease in dogs is the most common heart disorder, with up to 75 per cent of all cases leading to heart failure and death. Problems of heart failure and sudden death in Cavaliers at a critical time in the dog's life were often found to be due to a defect in the mitral heart valve. The condition of mitral valve disease (MVD) was first reported in 1987 and was then recognised to be widespread in the breed. Cavalier King Charles Spaniels have a strong breed predisposition for the development of heart disease, and typically show signs earlier in life and with a more rapid deterioration in health than other dog breeds. Males tend to develop mitral insufficiency earlier in life than females. Early death at between five and seven years was not unusual, and when other breeds with heart disease were shown to be living much longer, research was undertaken into this inherited disease. Very few Cavaliers were unaffected and treatment was only successful in extending life by a few years.

MVD is the result of degeneration and swelling of the valve tissue, with an inability for the valve to close fully. The valve in the heart between the left atrium and the main pumping chamber, the left ventricle, can no longer act as a seal. As the heart muscle contracts to propel blood round the body, some blood leaks back (regurgitation) instead of being propelled round the body. This leakage produces a noise known as a 'murmur' and this sound is looked for when the vet uses a stethoscope on the dog's chest. Sometimes a mild murmur is heard without any other signs (asymptomatic murmur), and then it is advised to repeat the examination every 6 to 12 months to look for deterioration. Often a murmur will not be detected until the Cavalier is at least a year old. MVD leads to congestive heart failure and sudden death, being life-threatening within one to three years of signs first appearing. As well as the stethoscope, chest X-rays, echocardiograms and the colour Doppler echocardiogram may be used for diagnosis.

The signs shown will be a dry, hacking cough and panting, a loss of appetite and often weight loss. As the blood flows back into the atrium on each heart beat, blood is held back in the lungs, leading to fluid flooding the lungs, a condition known as pulmonary oedema. Poor circulation may also be shown by weakness of the hind legs and a loss of the blood supply to the brain, resulting in collapse (syncope) similar to human fainting.

There is a strong hereditary factor, and breeding stock must be routinely screened for heart murmurs.

Sometimes the tricuspid valve on the opposite side of the heart is affected and the conditions are known as mitral/tricuspid valve dysplasia. Treatments with diuretics to remove fluid from the body and a number of specific heart drugs have proved successful in extending the life of affected Cavaliers.

as soon as the puppy's eyes open. More common – but still rare in Cavaliers – is a juvenile cataract that develops from six months of age but does not cause immediate blindness. Corneal dystrophy, where a whitish-grey deposit forms under the surface of the cornea, may be confused with the appearance of a lens cataract, but it is less serious.

Abnormalities of the eyelids, such as entropion, may be seen in the younger dogs as an inward-turning of the lid; the lashes rub on the eye ball surface (the cornea), causing irritation and eye watering. Other eyelid disorders – distichiasis and ectopic cilia – are of hereditary origins. Most such diseases are amenable to corrective surgery.

Conditions that affect the inside of the eye are more serious and can lead to blindness – the retina is the most important site of disease in the eye. Although not common, there is a group of inherited diseases known as progressive retinal atrophy (CPRA), which are known to occur in certain families. Blood tests are being used in some breeds to identify the faulty genes. Folding of the retina known as retinal dysplasia (RD) is also seen from time to time in Cavaliers. This condition only results in blindness if large areas of retina become detached. Milder RD is probably not a disability for the dog's eyesight.

HIP DYSPLASIA

As an inherited disease in many dogs, the breed average score for Cavaliers is at the lower level than many other working breeds. Hip dysplasia disease is a malformation of both the femoral head and acetabulum 'cup' of the hip, which results in lameness, pain and eventual arthritic changes. X-rays can be taken to measure the joint, and a score is awarded by a specialist who reads the photo plates. It is not a major problem in the breed, but anyone buying a puppy should enquire about the hip status of the parents before completing the purchase.

PATELLAR LUXATION
This condition, when the kneecap slips out of place, is often an inherited disease in smaller dog breeds, but it may also be the result of a torn ligament after jumping. The patellar or kneecap normally sits in a groove in the front of the stifle at the upper end of the femur bone. As many as 30 per cent of Cavaliers may have an unusually shallow groove, which makes it more possible for the patellar to dislocate and the dog

then looks distressed with his leg held up off the ground. Movement and massage by an experienced practitioner will often allow the patellar to slide back into place. Surgical operations are quite successful in curing the condition by settling the patellar more firmly in the groove.

SYRINGOMYELIA
This disease is a malformation of the hindbrain fluid system, with fluid-filled cavities found in the spinal cord of the upper neck. MRI screening tests are used from an early age to look for these defects, as they do not appear with X-rays. 'Fly catching' was the behaviour previously described for the behaviour, of twisting the neck and looking up in the air for an imaginary fly. The dog often

showed a scratching at the shoulder region, sometimes with painful screams when the head position was altered. Some affected dogs have a 'bunny hopping' gait.

The signs usually develop some time after six months of age; diagnosis can be confirmed by MRI scanning. Treatment at present is not very effective and only alleviates the symptoms, but a neurologist's opinion may be advised.

THROMBOCYTOPENIA
The tiny blood cells that are necessary for clot formation were found to be larger than normal in size, but less in number, in some King Charles Cavalier Spaniels subjected to routine blood tests in the USA. It is not known if this inherited condition is associated with disease in dogs. The blood-clotting disorder von Willebrand's disease has been found in the Cavalier, as in many other dog breeds, and it usually follows an inherited pattern when pedigrees of affected dogs are examined.

COMPLEMENTARY THERAPIES
There is a wide choice of treatments that can be given to dogs over and above the type of medical or surgical treatment that you might expect when attending a veterinary surgery. Some of

Complementary therapies are now more widely available and can prove beneficial.

these alternative treatments have proved to benefit dogs while others are better known for their effect on humans, where the placebo effect of an additional therapy has a strong influence on the benefit received.

PHYSIOTHERAPY

This is one of the longest-tested treatments used in injuries and after surgery on the limbs. Chartered physiotherapists and veterinary nurses who have studied the subject work under the direction of the vet will advise or apply procedures that will help mobility and recovery. Massage, heat, exercise or electrical stimulation are used to relieve pain, regain movement and restore muscle strength.

HYDROTHERAPY

Hydrotherapy is very popular, as many dogs enjoy swimming, and the use of water for the treatment of joint disease, injuries or for the maintenance of fitness and health is very effective.

ACUPUNCTURE

Derived from Chinese medicine, acupuncture has a long history of healing, involving the insertion of fine needles into specific locations in the body, known as 'acupuncture points'. The placing of the needles to stimulate nervous tissue is based on human charts and very good results have been reported when veterinary acupuncturists have selected suitable cases to treat using acupuncture.

REIKI

The laying on of a skilled operator's hands – Reiki – can have beneficial results. It is as equally convincing as acupuncture, and does not involve the dog tolerating needles in its body, but there are few qualified veterinary operators.

With good care and management, your Cavalier should live a long, happy and healthy life.

MAGNETIC THERAPY

Perhaps more questionable in observed results, magnetic therapy involves applying magnetic products to the dog, to relieve pain and increase mobility.

AROMATHERAPY

Aromatherapy also has a following; it involves the treatment of dogs with natural remedies, essential oils and plant extracts traditionally found in the wild.

PHYTOTHERAPY

Herbal medicine has proven benefits and there are an ever-increasing number of veterinary surgeons skilled in selecting appropriate plant products. Natural remedies are attractive to many users and provide a good alternative to many conventional veterinary treatments. Herbal drugs have become increasingly popular and their use is widespread, but licensing regulations and studies on interactions between herbal products and other veterinary medicines are still incomplete. One treatment for kennel cough – with liquorice, thyme and Echinacea – helped to cure a dog in 24 hours without antibiotics.

As with all alternative therapies, it is necessary to consult a person who has experience and specialised knowledge. Your Cavalier's vet should be informed of any treatments since there are contradictions between some veterinary medicines and other remedies. Acute and/or chronic liver damage occurred after ingestion of some Chinese herbs and care in the application of 'natural products' is advised.

THE CONTRIBUTORS

THE EDITOR
MARYANN HOGAN (Stavonga)
Maryann's interest in dogs began in earnest in 1975 with her first show Cavalier, a tricolour bitch called Fentiger Reseda (or 'Popsey' to her friends). Before long she had a small team of dogs and could be found up and down the country at Championship and Open Shows. Over the years she has owned all four colours, but, due to numbers, is restricted to particolours at this time

Maryann has participated in all aspects of dogdom, being involved in general Kennel Club and breed societies. She has been a breed club committee member for 27 years. She started judging Cavaliers in 1981 at Open Shows and in 1999 judged her first Championship show in the UK. Since then she has been lucky enough to judge at Championship level numerous times in the UK, France, Sweden, Australia and the USA. Maryann says, for her, there is no other breed than the Cavalier and she enjoys all aspects of dogdom – from exhibiting to fundraising, from breeding to judging. But most of all, she enjoys the love and companionship of her dogs.
See Chapter Seven: The Perfect Cavalier.

SHEILA HINDLE (Ellisiana)
Sheila purchased her first Cavalier in 1984, although she always had a dog in the house as a child. She started showing Cavaliers in 1987 and has five dogs in the studbook register, a dog with one reserve CC, and a bitch with a CC. A bitch she is showing at present has two reserve CCs. Sheila started judging Cavaliers in 1993, and awarded CCs for the first time in 2006.

Sheila has been secretary of the Humberside Cavalier King Charles Spaniel Club and is currently the secretary of the North East of England Toy Dog Society. She is also secretary of the Cleveland Dog Society, which is an all-breeds society, and she is a committee member of The Northern Cavalier Club.
See Chapter One: Getting to Know the Cavalier King Charles Spaniel.

JANE BOWDLER (Ttiweh)
Jane's mother, Amice Pitt, was one of the first pioneers of the Cavalier King Charles Spaniel, and so Jane was involved with the breed in its very early days. She can remember the first show Cavaliers and she used to join in grooming sessions with her mother. In those days, her mother kept over 60 dogs, specialising in Cavaliers and Chows. Jane was taken to all the shows when she was young, and got to know all the top breeders of the era. In 1946, Jane was presented with Daywell Roger by her mother, and she enjoyed all the excitement of campaigning a highly successful show dog.

Jane is a Championship judge and has judged at Crufts on two occasions: in 1964 and later at the Millennium show in 2000. She has travelled to many wonderful places on judging appointments and has made many good friends. Jane says that she owes a great deal to Cavaliers, and there is no other breed she would own.
See Chapter Two: The First Cavaliers.

BRIAN RIX & KEVAN BERRY (Ricksbury)
Brian and Kevan started showing Cavaliers in 1972, their foundation bitch being of Crisdig breeding, as they were renowned for their beautiful head, eyes and temperament. From Crisdig Saucy Sue the Ricksbury line was founded.

All Brian and Kevan's dogs are kept as pets, not in kennels, and they have always tried to keep numbers as low as possible. For that reason they are particularly proud of their contribution to the breed.

The first Champion to be made up under the Ricksbury prefix was Ch. Ricksbury Only Charm (1981) she was 2CC's short of the breed record – not bad for your first Champion! Since then Brian and Kevan have made up 20 Champions – all Blenheims. They have also made up five King Charles Champions (all tricolours).

Brian and Kevan are very proud to have bred some outstanding Cavaliers over the years, including but not restricted to, the current bitch breed record holder, Ch. Ricksbury Royal Temptress, with 28 CCs. She is the mother of six Champions – four of them UK Champions. Brian and Kevan have previously owned three earlier breed record holders.

Brian and Kevan have judged in many countries around the world, namely Australia Canada, Denmark, Finland, France, Ireland, New Zealand, Norway, Sweden, and the US. In addition, they have awarded CCs for Cavaliers at Crufts in 2005.

Brian and Kevan sum up their reasons for loving the breed in the following sentence: "At the end of the day our dogs are our lives, and the companionship and love they give us are without comparison."
See Chapter Three: A Cavalier for your Lifestyle.

LUCY KOSTER (Harana)
Lucy came from a 'doggie' family, having pet Poodles for many years. She was given a Blenheim boy when she was nine, and quickly got bitten by the showing bug.

She then bought a Ch. Alansmere Aquarius granddaughter, from whom she bred a litter in 1983, producing her first Crufts qualifier in 1984.

Lucy enjoyed reasonable success with particolours, including breeding Ch. Harana Christa at Toraylac – one of the top-winning bitches of the time. However, she had always had a hankering for whole colours and a black and tan boy eventually arrived in August 1985. He went on to become Lucy's first Champion – Ch. Knight Magic at Harana – made up in 1987. He, along with Salador Copperglint at Harana, became the foundation for all her present whole colours.

Lucy's first homebred Champion, Rockstar, was made up in 1991, followed by Too Darn Hot in 1995 – the only ruby dog to win BOB at Crufts. Nina Simone was made up in 1998, becoming the breed's youngest black and tan bitch Champion. Minnelli and Good Golly Miss Molly both gained their crowns in 2003 – the first ruby bitch Champions for 12 years. The following year, Starman becoming the first black and tan dog Champion for 11 years.

Dogs carrying the Harana affix have won a total of 37 CCs and 46 Reserve CCs plus numerous

Best of Colour awards in the Parent Clubs' yearly points trophies. There have been many overseas Champions carrying the Harana affix, including American, Australian and European title-holders.

Lucy's first judging appointment was in 1988, and she first awarded Challenge Certificates in 1997. She has also judged in Ireland, Europe, America and New Zealand.
See Chapter Four: The New Arrival

LINDA FLYNN (Linjato)
Dogs have played a big part in Linda's life since her early childhood. Her first Cavaliers were from the famous Maxholt kennels, which introduced her to the world of showing along with a bitch, Cinola Modern Girl of Linjato, from the late Barbara Evans. In 1984 Linda went to live in Belgium with her husband, where another Cavalier from the UK joined her family – Cinola Tara of Linjato. Both the Cinola bitches founded the Linjato line.

Linda began showing Cavaliers very successfully in Europe, with Modern Girl gaining many titles and becoming an international, Dutch, Belgian and Luxembourg Champion. She began judging in 1986 and then returned to England in 1989. She awarded CCs in the UK for the first time in 1999 and then in Ireland in 2008. She has also judged at Championship show level in the US, Canada, Australia, France, Holland and Belgium.

Linda has bred and owned several CC winners and has also bred one of the UK's top sires, Linjato Ace of Base JW, who sired more than 20 Champions worldwide.

Linda has been a committee member of the Humberside Cavalier King Charles Spaniel Club since 1994 and is currently the club's secretary and its rescue coordinator. She enjoys all aspects of the dog world, from organising shows and seminars to rescue fun days, but most of all she loves playing with her Cavaliers in her garden or walking them along the beach close to her home.
Chapter Five: The Best of Care.

JULIA BARNES
Julia has owned and trained a number of different dog breeds, and is a puppy socialiser for Dogs for the Disabled. A former journalist, she has written many books, including several on dog training and behaviour. Julia is indebted to Maryann Hogan for her specialist knowledge on Cavalier training and behaviour.
See Chapter Six: Training and Socialisation.

DICK LANE BScFRAgSFRCVS
Dick qualified from the Royal Veterinary College in 1953 and then spent most of his time in veterinary practice in Warwickshire. He had a particular interest in assistance dogs: working for the Guide Dogs for the Blind Association and more recently for Dogs for the Disabled as a founder trustee. Dick has been awarded a Fellowship of the Royal College of Veterinary Surgeons and a Fellowship of the Royal Agricultural Societies. He has recently completed an Honours BSc in Applied Animal Behaviour and Training, awarded by the University of Hull.
See Chapter Eight: Happy and Healthy.

USEFUL ADDRESSES

KENNEL & BREED CLUBS

UK
The Kennel Club
1 Clarges Street, London, W1J 8AB
Tel: 0870 606 6750
Fax: 0207 518 1058
Web: www.the-kennel-club.org.uk

To obtain up-to-date contact information for the following breed clubs, please contact the Kennel Club:
- Cavalier King Charles Spaniel Club
- Eastern Counties Cavalier King Charles Spaniel Society
- Humberside Cavalier King Charles Spaniel Club
- Midland Cavalier King Charles Spaniel Club
- Northern Cavalier King Charles Spaniel Society
- Northern Ireland Cavalier King Charles Spaniel Club
- Scottish Cavalier King Charles Spaniel Club
- South and West Wales Cavalier King Charles Spaniel Club
- Southern Cavalier King Charles Spaniel Club
- West of England Cavalier King Charles Spaniel Club

USA
American Kennel Club (AKC)
5580 Centerview Drive,
Raleigh, NC 27606, USA.
Tel: 919 233 9767
Fax: 919 233 3627
Email: info@akc.org
Web: www.akc.org

United Kennel Club (UKC)
100 E Kilgore Rd, Kalamazoo,
MI 49002 5584, USA.
Tel: 269 343 9020
Fax: 269 343 7037
Web:www.ukcdogs.com/

American Cavalier King Charles Spaniel Club, Inc.
Web: http://www.ackcsca.org/

For contact details of regional clubs, please contact the American Cavalier King Charles Spaniel Club.

AUSTRALIA
Australian National Kennel Council (ANKC)
The Australian National Kennel Council is the administrative body for pure breed canine affairs in Australia. It does not, however, deal directly with dog exhibitors, breeders or judges. For information pertaining to breeders, clubs or shows, please contact the relevant State or Territory Controlling Body.

Dogs Australian Capital Teritory
PO Box 815, Dickson ACT 2602
Tel: (02) 6241 4404
Fax: (02) 6241 1129

Email: administrator@dogsact.org.au
Web: www.dogsact.org.au

Dogs New South Wales
PO Box 632, St Marys, NSW 1790
Tel: (02) 9834 3022 or 1300 728 022 (NSW Only)
Fax: (02) 9834 3872
Email: info@dogsnsw.org.au
Web: www.dogsnsw.org.au

Dogs Northern Territory
PO Box 37521, Winnellie NT 0821
Tel: (08) 8984 3570
Fax: (08) 8984 3409
Email: admin@dogsnt.com.au
Web: www.dogsnt.com.au

Dogs Queensland
PO Box 495, Fortitude Valley Qld 4006
Tel: (07) 3252 2661
Fax: (07) 3252 3864
Email: info@dogsqueensland.org.au
Web: www.dogsqueensland.org.au

Dogs South Australia
PO Box 844
Prospect East SA 5082
Tel: (08) 8349 4797
Fax: (08) 8262 5751
Email: info@dogssa.com.au
Web: www.dogssa.com.au

Tasmanian Canine Association Inc
The Rothman Building
PO Box 116
Glenorchy Tas 7010
Tel: (03) 6272 9443
Fax: (03) 6273 0844
Email: tca@iprimus.com.au
Web: www.tasdogs.com

Dogs Victoria
Locked Bag K9
Cranbourne VIC 3977
Tel: (03)9788 2500
Fax: (03) 9788 2599
Email: office@dogsvictoria.org.au
Web: www.dogsvictoria.org.au

Dogs Western Australia
PO Box 1404
Canning Vale WA 6970
Tel: (08) 9455 1188
Fax: (08) 9455 1190
Email: k9@dogswest.com
Web: www.dogswest.com

INTERNATIONAL
Fédération Cynologique Internationalé (FCI)/World Canine Organisation
Place Albert 1er, 13, B-6530 Thuin,
Belgium.
Tel: +32 71 59.12.38
Fax: +32 71 59.22.29
Web: www.fci.be/

TRAINING AND BEHAVIOUR

UK
Association of Pet Dog Trainers
PO Box 17, Kempsford, GL7 4WZ
Telephone: 01285 810811
Email: APDToffice@aol.com
Web: http://www.apdt.co.uk

Association of Pet Behaviour Counsellors
PO BOX 46, Worcester, WR8 9YS
Telephone: 01386 751151
Fax: 01386 750743
Email: info@apbc.org.uk
Web: http://www.apbc.org.uk/

USA
Association of Pet Dog Trainers
101 North Main Street, Suite 610
Greenville, SC 29601, USA.
Tel: 1 800 738 3647
Email: information@apdt.com
Web: www.apdt.com/

American College of Veterinary Behaviorists
College of Veterinary Medicine, 4474 Tamu,
Texas A&M University
College Station, Texas 77843-4474
Web: http://dacvb.org/

American Veterinary Society of Animal Behavior
Web: www.avsabonline.org/

AUSTRALIA
APDT Australia Inc
PO Box 3122, Bankstown Square, NSW 2200.
Email: secretary@apdt.com.au
Web: www.apdt.com.au

Canine Behaviour
For details of regional behvaiourists, contact the relevant State or Territory Controlling Body.

ACTIVITIES

UK
Agility Club
http://www.agilityclub.co.uk/

British Flyball Association
PO Box 990, Doncaster, DN1 9FY
Telephone: 01628 829623
Email: secretary@flyball.org.uk
Web: http://www.flyball.org.uk/

Working Trials
36 Elwyndene Road, March, Cambridgeshire,
PE15 9RL.
www.workingtrials.co.uk

USA
North American Dog Agility Council
P.O. Box 1206, Colbert,
OK 74733, USA.
Web: www.nadac.com/

North American Flyball Association, Inc.
1333 West Devon Avenue, #512
Chicago, IL 60660
Tel/Fax: 800 318 6312
Email: flyball@flyball.org
Web: www.flyball.org/

AUSTRALIA
Agility Dog Association of Australia
ADAA Secretary, PO Box 2212,
Gailes, QLD 4300, Australia.
Tel: 0423 138 914
Email: admin@adaa.com.au
Web: www.adaa.com.au/

NADAC Australia (North American Dog Agility Council - Australian Division)
12 Wellman Street, Box Hill South, Victoria 3128, Australia.
Email: shirlene@nadacaustralia.com
Web: www.nadacaustralia.com/

Australian Flyball Association
PO Box 4179, Pitt Town, NSW 2756
Tel: 0407 337 939
Email: info@flyball.org.au
Web: www.flyball.org.au/

INTERNATIONAL

World Canine Freestyle Organisation
P.O. Box 350122, Brooklyn, NY 11235-2525, USA
Tel: (718) 332-8336
Fax: (718) 646-2686
Email: wcfodogs@aol.com
Web: www.worldcaninefreestyle.org

HEALTH

UK
Alternative Veterinary Medicine Centre
Chinham House, Stanford in the Vale,
Oxfordshire, SN7 8NQ
Tel: 01367 710324
Fax: 01367 718243
Web: www.alternativevet.org/

British Small Animal Veterinary Association
Woodrow House, 1 Telford Way,
Waterwells Business Park, Quedgeley,
Gloucestershire, GL2 2AB
Tel: 01452 726700
Fax: 01452 726701
Email: customerservices@bsava.com
Web: http://www.bsava.com/

Royal College of Veterinary Surgeons
Belgravia House, 62-64 Horseferry Road,
London, SW1P 2AF
Tel: 0207 222 2001
Fax: 0207 222 2004
Email: admin@rcvs.org.uk
Web: www.rcvs.org.uk

USA
American Holistic Veterinary Medical Association
2218 Old Emmorton Road
Bel Air, MD 21015
Tel: 410 569 0795
Fax 410 569 2346
Email: office@ahvma.org
Web: www.ahvma.org/

American Veterinary Medical Association
1931 North Meacham Road, Suite 100,
Schaumburg, IL 60173-4360, USA.
Tel: 800 248 2862
Fax: 847 925 1329
Web: www.avma.org

American College of Veterinary Surgeons
19785 Crystal Rock Dr, Suite 305
Germantown, MD 20874, USA.
Tel: 301 916 0200
Toll Free: 877 217 2287
Fax: 301 916 2287
Email: acvs@acvs.org
Web: www.acvs.org/

AUSTRALIA
Australian Holistic Vets
Web: www.ahv.com.au/

Australian Small Animal Veterinary Association
40/6 Herbert Street, St Leonards, NSW 2065, Australia.
Tel: 02 9431 5090
Fax: 02 9437 9068
Email: asava@ava.com.au
Web: www.asava.com.au

Australian Veterinary Association
Unit 40, 6 Herbert Street, St Leonards, NSW 2065, Australia.
Tel: 02 9431 5000
Fax: 02 9437 9068
Web: www.ava.com.au

Australian College Veterinary Scientists
Building 3, Garden City Office Park,
2404 Logan Road, Eight Mile Plains,
Queensland 4113, Australia.
Tel: 07 3423 2016
Fax: 07 3423 2977
Email: admin@acvs.org.au
Web: http://acvsc.org.au

ASSISTANCE DOGS

Canine Partners
Mill Lane, Heyshott, Midhurst,
, GU29 0ED
Tel: 08456 580480
Fax: 08456 580481
Web: www.caninepartners.co.uk

Dogs for the Disabled
The Frances Hay Centre, Blacklocks Hill,
Banbury, Oxon, OX17 2BS

Tel: 01295 252600
Web: www.dogsforthedisabled.org

Guide Dogs for the Blind Association
Burghfield Common, Reading, RG7 3YG
Tel: 01189 835555
Fax: 01189 835433
Web: www.guidedogs.org.uk/

Hearing Dogs for Deaf People
The Grange, Wycombe Road, Saunderton,
Princes Risborough, Bucks, HP27 9NS
Tel: 01844 348100
Fax: 01844 348101
Web: www.hearingdogs.org.uk

Pets as Therapy
3a Grange Farm Cottages, Wycombe Road,
Saunderton, Princes Risborough,
Bucks, HP27 9NS
Tel: 01845 345445
Fax: 01845 550236
Web: http://www.petsastherapy.org/

Support Dogs
21 Jessops Riverside, Brightside Lane,
Sheffield, S9 2RX
Tel: 01142 617800
Fax: 01142 617555
Email: supportdogs@btconnect.com
Web: www.support-dogs.org.uk

USA
Therapy Dogs International
88 Bartley Road, Flanders, NJ 07836,.
Tel: 973 252 9800
Fax: 973 252 7171
Email: tdi@gti.net
Web: www.tdi-dog.o

Therapy Dogs Inc.
P.O. Box 20227, Cheyenne, WY 82003.
Tel: 307 432 0272.
Fax: 307-638-2079　.
Web: www.therapydogs.com

Delta Society - Pet Partners
875 124th Ave NE, Suite 101 • Bellevue, WA 98005 USA.
Email: info@DeltaSociety.org
Web: www.deltasociety.org

Comfort Caring Canines
8135 Lare Street, Philadelphia, PA 19128.
Email: ccc@comfortcaringcanines.org
Web: www.comfortcaringcanines.org/

AUSTRALIA
AWARE Dogs Australia, Inc
PO Box 883, Kuranda, Queensland, 488, Australia.
Tel: 07 4093 8152
Web: www.awaredogs.org.au/

Delta Society — Therapy Dogs
Web: www.deltasociety.com.au